THE PROBLEM WAS ME

THOMAS GAGLIANO
With Abraham J. Twerski, MD

THE PROBLEM WAS ME

A Guide to Self-Awareness, Compassion, and Awareness

THOMAS GAGLIANO
With Abraham J. Twerski, MD

Gentle Path
P R E S S

Carefree, Arizona

Gentle Path Press
P.O. Box 3172
Carefree, Arizona 85377
www.gentlepath.com

First Edition: 2011

For more information regarding our publications, please contact-
Gentle Path Press at 1-800-708-1796 (toll-free U.S. only).

Book edited by Rebecca Post, Marianne Harkin
Book designed by Serena Castillo
Typesetting by Kinne Design

ISBN: 978-0-9826505-7-8

Names of people and situations described in this book have been changed
to protect the anonymity of the people involved.

Contents

Acknowledgments

I am grateful to and proud of my wife and children for their willingness and courage in allowing this book to come to fruition. Their faith that this book could help others was a vital source of strength for me. A special thanks to Tony, who has always been there to cheer me on, especially when I felt this book would never become a reality. Tony, along with Robert and Joe, supplied me with the support I needed to keep going, especially when my warden was telling me I would never be able to follow this through. Thanks to everyone in my support system who have journeyed along with me as we have silenced our wardens' commands together. These people have always been an important part of my life, and they are important contributors to this book.

Preface

By Abraham J. Twerski, M.D.

When I was in psychiatric training and assigned to report on Thomas Mann's *The Magic Mountain*, I was deeply impressed by Mann's insights. I recall asking my professor if Thomas Mann was a physician. His response, "Don't be silly. No doctor could be that sensitive."

There is truth to the professor's statement. Scientific medical training so saturates the left brain that the right brain, the part that receives and develops feelings, is overwhelmed. The occupational hazard of being a physician is that we may lose some measure of sensitivity. Tom Gagliano is neither a psychiatrist nor a psychologist, but he is a sensitive human being who holds valuable psychological insights gained from life experiences rather than from books and lectures. Tom's words are laden with emotion.

In one of my earlier books, *Addictive Thinking*, I described the unique thought processes of an addict. These same processes occur in non-addicts but are exaggerated in addicts. Tom Gagliano speaks from the vantage point of a recovering addict, but everyone can identify with the emotions he describes. He points out the destructive impact that early experiences can have on a person's life, but if you are aware of these early obstacles then you can take proper steps to free yourself from their stranglehold. *The Problem Was Me* is not only a self-help book, but a valuable textbook for mental health professionals.

Introduction

By Thomas Gagliano

*Not until I stopped denying my own past and began sharing
my wounds, did I allow myself to be loved by other people.*

ഇ)രു

You do not have to be addicted to drugs or alcohol to benefit
from this book. This book can help you with whatever distraction you
are using to avoid whatever it is you should be doing. Before the rapid
proliferation of computers, video games, satellite TV, and cell phones,
we had fewer choices for acting out our compulsions. Now with the
explosive growth of digital devices, we can gamble, shop, play video
games, and view pornography with a click of a mouse or by pressing a
button on a remote.

While I am not a licensed therapist, I have gained great insight
through my own process of healing from the destructive behaviors
in my life. In addition, I have coached many people who have been
crippled by their own internal demons. Having faced my own demons,
I know how it feels to be overwhelmed, hopeless, and completely
paralyzed with fear.

With the help of Twelve Step programs, group sessions, organized retreats, workshops, and sponsors, I discovered the way to a better
life and how to help others find their own paths. It was not until I
opened myself to change that I began to transform from the person
who once isolated himself from others to a man who has become rich
with the wonders of life and the love of family and friends. I found
peace and my own spirituality.

Healing is an ongoing process of self-determination and self-
discipline. While the rewards are not always immediate, beautiful gifts
await if you are patient and can take direction. As I healed internally,

1

a need emerged to share how I did it with others. I began to help people from all walks of life, including rabbis, priests, doctors, plumbers, housewives, computer technicians, CEOs, therapists, sales people, and engineers. Because we could identify with each other's struggles, the people I coached opened a part of their lives to me that had been off limits to others and even to themselves. As I helped them face their biggest fears, I was encouraged to face my own shortcomings and the obstacles I needed to overcome in shaking off my personal demons. Not until I stopped denying my own past and began sharing my wounds did I allow myself to be loved by other people.

Some of the people I have helped have shared my philosophies with their therapists. After sharing my insight with some of the professionals I met with, they began to adopt my methods in treating their own patients. This book is filled with nuggets of wisdom that are invaluable and affirming. It explores the underlying reasons why we behave the way we do. The book is designed to be a reference tool. You could turn to any chapter and find helpful information on ways to deal with life on life's terms.

The encouragement from the people who allowed me to help them has inspired me to write this book. *The Problem Was Me* contains the tools gained from my personal struggle with compulsions and applies a methodology as exemplified by Abraham Twerski. Through the experiences, insights, and the wisdom I have gained in my journey in life, combined with Dr. Twerski's professional wisdom, this book can help those with destructive behaviors as well as supply others with a blueprint to give their children the love denied to many of them. So many people feel they were denied of loving behaviors from their parents. This book will also bring an understanding to family and friends who seek to prevent themselves or their loved ones from continuing on a path of self-destruction.

The common problems we face are from unhealed childhood wounds that have remained buried and have haunted us. Only when we permit the window into our past to be opened, exposing the core of our adult difficulties, can we begin the healing process. Today, I am aware of how deeply I was imprisoned by childhood wounds and how negative voices from the past disturb me today.

Throughout *The Problem Was Me,* I refer to the warden, an imaginary person with a bat, who sat on my shoulder. Whenever someone made me feel defective, he would come out swinging. The warden instilled in me a peculiar definition of intimacy. Intimacy meant pain, and should be avoided. The warden was trying to protect me from getting too close to anyone. This imaginary guy on my shoulder has been with me a long time, as far back as I can remember. His motive for using the bat was to take a swing at me if I ever got the idea that I deserved to be happy or if I stumbled and made a mistake. He permitted me no margin for error.

The warden becomes the little voice inside our heads that won't go away. The little voice keeps us imprisoned by reminding us of the intrusive messages we received in childhood over and over again. Childhood wounds are reopened, isolating us from others. In many ways, we play roles in our lives that can bring harmful consequences to others and to ourselves. We wear masks to hide who we really are. The little voice makes us feel ashamed and unworthy. We become self-centered causing us to feel that we have the right to something regardless of the harm it causes others. We call this destructive entitlement.

The warden's voice inside our head repeats that we do not deserve to be happy. His voice leads us to sabotage happiness when it comes our way. He is so powerful that even though he imprisons us to destructive roles in our lives, we listen to him.

What roles in your life did your warden command you to play?

1. *Caretaking Role*—Taking care of the world can be tiring, yet the warden will not allow you to let go of taking care of others.

2. *Victim Role*—The warden's voice exempts you from taking responsibility in your life. All your problems are caused by your spouse, employer, children, parents, or others.

3. *Transparent Role*—The warden warns against sharing feelings; no one wants to hear how you feel.

4. *Defiant Role*—The warden creates a voice that directs you to disagree with everyone, especially those of authority.

5. *Compliant Role*—The warden creates a voice that directs you to agree with everyone. How they feel about you matters more than you feel about yourself.

6. *Angry Role*—The warden forbids against admitting to mistakes, so you use your anger to always prove you are right. How you hurt others reflects your inner pain.

7. *Underachieving Role*—The warden warns that failing is so painful that it is not worth even trying.

8. *Controlling Role*—The warden warns us that any process we cannot control will not end positively; therefore, everyone must act and think the way we want them to.

The warden keeps us emotionally shackled and orders us to keep our doors locked, so no one can enter. This book provides the key to unlocking the locked door and allowing happiness into our lives.

There are three essential strategies to healing that will free us from the chains of our childhood wounds. These include awareness, action, and maintenance. First, we must become aware of what is broken inside so we know what to fix. Second, positive actions allow us to see our true responsibility in each situation and help to stop the voice inside of us from directing our behavior in negative ways. We discover that if we do what we always did, then we'll get what we always got. As we start to act in healthier ways, the distorted view we have of others and ourselves begins to melt away. Eventually, through positive actions, our perceptions and dynamics change, bringing more peace into our lives. Third, maintaining positive actions in an environment where there is group support will stop the destructive inner voice from coming back to take charge of our behavior again.

If you do not have *awareness*, you cannot take *action*.

If you cannot take *action*, there is nothing to *maintain*.

One of my most rewarding feelings is the gratitude I receive from a spouse or family member of someone I have coached. Once the healing begins, the love returns to their marriage and is passed down to their children. This miracle, which is reflected in my own marriage, fills me with overwhelming joy.

Sometimes we act in ways that do not always make sense as we hurt ourselves and others. We feel compelled to listen to the destructive inner voice in our heads. Making sense of our actions is like figuring out a jigsaw puzzle. This book will allow you to put the puzzle pieces together. If you are still unsure if this book could help you, take a few minutes to ask yourself the following questions.

- Do you tend to focus on the shortcomings of others to avoid looking at yourself?

- Do you say yes to people because saying no is too painful?

- Do you feel like you are carrying the burden of the world on your shoulders and are powerless to let it go?

- Do you feel victimized by people or circumstances in your life?

- Do you have problems trusting any process that you are not in control of?

- When you make a mistake, do you feel shame so strong it overwhelms you?

- Do you take the time to celebrate the victories (successes) in your life, or do you beat yourself up over your failures?

- Do you feel comfortable being intimate, or do you avoid intimacy?

- Are you most comfortable being isolated from others even though you realize that avoiding social contact keeps you locked in depression and self-pity?

- When you get angry, do you terrify the people around you, or do you suppress, ignore, or stuff anger?

- Do you feel invisible in your relationships?

- In social settings, do you feel either superior or inferior to others, rather than feeling like you belong?

- Do you always have to be right, even if you push people away?

- Do you have destructive behaviors that hurt you or others, but still feel entitled to continue your addictive behavior?

- Do you give away your power to others by letting them determine how you feel about yourself?

- Do you make up stories in your mind about the way others feel about you, but don't have the courage to tell them how you feel?

- Are there tasks you must do, but are paralyzed to start?

- Do you want help, but aren't able to take that first step and don't know why?

If you answered yes to any of the questions, this book is for you. Each of us can benefit from a better understanding of how childhood wounds mold the person we are today. Some addicts who have been sober for a long time may continue to lead tormented, angry lives. This book will explore why and how to make positive changes. The intention of this book is not to bash our caregivers or parents. Rather, it is to understand the effects of these messages given to us in childhood that impact our lives at this moment. Today I can fail at times, but it does not mean I am a failure. I can make mistakes, but it does not mean I am a mistake. The words expressed throughout this book are from my heart. It is my fervent wish to bring hope to those imprisoned by a wounded past.

Chapter One: Damaged Goods

Something had to be wrong with me or my parents
wouldn't act the way they did.

ɞᴄʁ

As a child in a family filled with dysfunction, my belief system told me that I was the cause of the insanity within my home. When my needs were not satisfied as a child, rather than acknowledging that something might be wrong with my parents, I believed that something must be wrong with me. My father was often away from home while I was growing up. My mother was always trying to locate him. As the oldest child, I became a caretaker for my mother. One night she threatened suicide. She told me to find my father or she was going to carry out her threat. She held a long, sharp knife used by my father to cut meat. She pointed the sharp end at her stomach, threatening to stab herself if I did not phone my father immediately and get him home. I was about ten years old. The first phone call I made was to my grandmother. She told me where I could find my father. My hands trembled as I dialed the number. When I heard his voice I started to sob, pleading with him to come quickly.

When my father arrived home, I noticed that even he was scared that my mother was about to do something crazy. I kept my eyes glued to the knife in my mother's hands, saying to myself, *Please put the knife down.* Instead of yelling or screaming like he often did, my father tried to calm her down. As he tried to talk her out of committing suicide, I heard him saying, "What about the children? Who will take care of them?" My mother replied, "I don't care about the kids. I only want you." Eventually, my mother put down the knife. It would take me another twenty-five years to acknowledge that on that night I also become a victim. Something inside me died when I heard those hurtful words of hers. Those words, like an earthquake, cracked the very foundation of my belief system.

That traumatic night set off a chain reaction of events in my life. The deep emotional scars would imprison me in self-destructive thoughts from adolescence through my adult and married life. In fairness to Mother, my father broke her heart. She was on medication at the time and was not in a great state of mind. Unfortunately, this information does not make a difference to a young child. Whatever the reasons, the message was clear. From that day forward, I felt like damaged goods. If my own mother did not love me, then something was definitely wrong with me.

Deep and painful childhood wounds can tie us to a lifetime of isolation and loneliness. As a result of our childhood, we may not have physical wounds visible on the outside. However, our emotional wounds might be more difficult to detect and heal. All of the harmful messages we receive in our lives and the resulting painful wounds wreak havoc in our adult lives. They affect our thoughts, judgment, and behavior. They block our path to peace and happiness. We develop a false belief system based on these early wounds about the world and ourselves. From these beliefs spring the voice of someone I call the warden or the damaging little voice inside our heads. Any time happiness approaches, the warden uses his power to push others away and keep us playing the damaging roles that he tells us to play.

As a child, I learned that needing and depending on others was a sign of weakness. Like a wounded animal, I was afraid to let anyone get close. I felt inadequate, unloved, rejected, defective, and shut down in shame. I behaved irrationally to avoid the pain. Until I became aware of my wounds and found the courage to heal them, it was impossible to experience intimacy or have a relationship with a Higher Power. I learned early on that it was unsafe to trust anyone.

Destructive behaviors helped to relieve the pain and to medicate my discomfort. My distorted outlook on life was further obscured by a belief system contaminated with faulty and unhealthy messages. The core of that belief system was responsible for my victim thinking. On one hand, this corrupted belief system cultivated feelings of self-pity and a destructive entitlement to act out. On the other hand, it failed to point out the consequences of self-destructive thoughts and behavior. The truth is, I was a victim as a child. Terrible things happened to me as a child. While I was not accountable for what occurred during childhood, I was responsible for allowing this victim mentality to continue into my adult life. The little voice inside my head kept telling me that the world owed me something, thereby creating unrealistic expectations and a sense of entitlement.

When I began to recognize what was going on inside, I focused on positive changes to improve my overall attitude. I needed to delete the old messages that fueled my destructive behaviors. I surrounded myself with the right people. These are people who hold me accountable and bring me back when my ego gets in the way. They encourage me when I lose hope and urge me to live without false pretenses. In addition, these people accept me for who I am even when I cannot accept myself. These people comprise my support group today. The messages I received as a child distorted my thinking, so I needed to develop a solution and new belief system to counter my negative way of thinking. It was not until I began to participate in meetings and therapist-led support groups that my growth and healing would begin. These experiences galvanized a new way of thinking about life, and motivated me to work through childhood traumas and destructive behaviors that had been holding me back. Much of the credit for my internal growth comes from several therapists who guided me through some of the most difficult times in my life. I supplemented this personal healing by attending couples' meetings, which gave me additional strength and hope in healing difficult family wounds.

Although I was a successful businessman, husband, and father, I needed to wear a mask. I was never comfortable in the company of others and masked feelings of inadequacy, defectiveness, and loneliness. No material wealth could fill this void. My emptiness drove me into destructive behaviors, even at the risk of losing everything and everyone I love. I began to listen to this voice inside my head instead of trusting people. I felt insane, out of control, and scared. The warden's condemning voice was loud, malicious, and repetitive. It told me over and over again that I was unworthy, unlovable, and never good enough. No amount of money or love from my beautiful family could comfort me from the pain. When alone, the negative voice would dominate my thinking. As much as I tried to ignore the pain from early childhood, I could not. I had a void deep within me, preventing me from experiencing any true sense of fulfillment. Eventually, I realized that my insanity would continue until I accepted the truth about my life.

I had to start at the beginning to fully understand the origin of my pain that had a stranglehold on my life. Once I acknowledged my difficult childhood, I began to see myself as a discouraged person who needed help, not the evil man who deserved to be punished. When I took off my mask, I discovered that most of my fears were of my own making.

Chapter Two: I Am the Problem

If I managed my business like I managed my life,
I would have gone bankrupt. I may even have fired myself.

ℰↄႩ

Sometimes we need to revisit the past before we can move beyond our current struggles. Going back allows us to revisit those early childhood traumas and discover the origin of the pain, which we continue to drag along with us. We go through this process so we can grow in self-awareness, self-compassion, and self-acceptance. The goal is not to blame others, but to experience forgiveness and healing.

As a child, I put my parents on a pedestal, certain that they would protect and provide for me and my brothers. I was the oldest of four boys. To the outside world, my mother appeared warm and kind. Many people admired my father because he was charming and successful; he had a great sense of humor and was confident. It was a different story behind closed doors. Chaos and drama ensued at home as my parents fought loudly. They never said anything nice to each other. These fights usually ended with my father leaving with his suitcase while my mother stayed behind crying. My mother continually told me what a horrible person my father was. How I felt became dependent on how well I could please her. If she was happy, I was happy too. But, most of the time, she was very sad. It seemed like my mother wanted me to fix something inside of her that I didn't have the power to fix. My father's vices included alcohol, gambling, and womanizing.

My brothers and I were just added baggage for my father. He said to my mother, "Do you realize how much money I would have if I didn't have to feed these kids?" These words affected my self-esteem greatly. I blamed myself for everything. I truly believed that something was wrong with me. My inner voice suggested that none of this would have happened if I had been a better person and son. I was defective and damaged.

At an early age, my father would bring my brothers and me to the racetrack. We cheered for the horses he placed bets on as if they meant everything to us. At home, my father would bet money on football, baseball, and basketball games. We would then cheer those teams with the same intensity. He enjoyed the way we rallied for his teams while we enjoyed the attention he gave us. Gambling was his world. Sometimes he gave us a few dollars each to gamble with. That enabled us to get even closer to his world.

I hated my father and yearned for his acceptance at the same time. I craved his attention and wanted him to be proud of me—or at least show me that I mattered in some way. I decided if I wanted him to notice me, I would need to become successful and make lots of money. At an early age, I equated happiness and success with money. I was enterprising even at age eleven. I bought soda for 10 cents a can and sold it at local softball games for a quarter. I would pocket $20 to $40 each day.

An inner voice told me if I could not make my mother happy, I was a bad son. I felt responsible for my mother's happiness. She wanted to hurt my father the way he hurt her. One time she took me to a hotel to catch my father with another woman. I was about ten years old at the time. I knocked on the hotel room door and a woman opened it. My father was right behind her. When he saw me, he started to scream and yell at my mother, who was standing beside me in the hall. She shouted back. Other guests stepped out of their rooms into the hallway to witness this insane scene. I was so afraid and ashamed. I just wanted to be told everything would be fine. Instead, my parents acted like I wasn't there. Feelings of isolation and shame would carry into my adult life. The shame of being an invisible child, whose feelings did not matter, would influence my behaviors later on.

My mother always dressed provocatively. I remember men staring at her inappropriately. I would keep my head down, too ashamed to look up. I just wanted to disappear. I once told my mother how I felt. She went ballistic saying, "Don't you ever tell me how to

12

dress. It's none of your business! Your father put these thoughts into your head!"

My parents rarely said anything nice to each another. My father was kind until he drank. Then he would become unbearable. His remarks were very hurtful. As bad as it was, I always wanted my parents to stay together. I prayed it would work out. My father would only do something nice for my mother on her birthday or Christmas if I forced him. I would fight with him to get money so I could buy my mother a gift, seemingly from him. He would spoil the surprise by getting drunk or attaching a nasty comment to the gift. My father's attempts to sabotage everything she did made things difficult. Whenever we were ready to leave from somewhere my father would address my brothers and me by saying, "Let's go, girls." Happiness was never a comfortable feeling for him. He was hurting inside and he was hurting those around him as well. His inner voice, like mine, told him he did not deserve to be happy.

When his drinking got worse, he became physically abusive. I spent many nights sitting at the top of the stairs waiting for him to come home from work. I worried about my mother's safety. If he was drunk, I didn't know what he might do to her. When my father did not come home right from work, I knew he was going to come home drunk. That meant trouble. There were nights they shouted at each other as I stood shaking uncontrollably at the top of the stairs. One time, I heard a slap and a terrified scream from my mother. I flew down the stairs and stood in front of my mother to protect her. My father hit me a few times and knocked me away. My mother then hit him. The next day my father told me he was sorry and to forget it ever happened. I wished I could.

In the late 1960s and early 1970s, I attended a Catholic grammar school. Students who got into trouble were called into the principal's office. After the door was shut, the principal would broadcast the student being beaten on the intercom system so the whole school could hear. All the students were terrified of being called into the office. When I was in the third grade, the principal called a girl who sat in front of me to the office. As I sat behind her, I saw a stream of urine coming down her seat into the aisle. She began to cry from embarrassment.

We found out later that her mother was just picking her up to go to the doctor.

In the seven years I attended grammar school, I had four terrible experiences. The first was a beating I got from a young priest because my hair was too long. The second was a fight with a kid in school; I had made his lip bleed. The teacher brought me from room to room while smacking me in the face in front of each class. The third episode occurred when I was waiting for the school bus to take me home. One of the other kids threw a snowball at the bus. The next thing I knew, a nun was washing my face with a handful of snow. She assumed I threw the snowball. It wasn't the snow that bothered me, but the humiliation of the other kids laughing at me when the nun left.

The fourth and worst experience was in confession. I hadn't gone to church for a long time. As I confessed this to the priest, he became upset. He called me an animal and said I should live in a jungle with the other animals. He went on and on about how sick I made him and what a disgrace I was. I reached this conclusion: If this man represents God then who needs God? To me, these experiences were proof that I wasn't a good person, and I deserved punishment. The warden or my inner voice emphasized this belief whenever possible.

As I grew older, sports became my stress reliever. I always felt the need to win. Losing meant that I was a failure. I could not handle that. I also had to be right all the time. During an argument, I had to get the last word in. I needed people to see things my way. The terrifying thought of being wrong made me feel defective. I never let anyone get close. If someone was getting too close or becoming attached to me, I would find ways to distance myself by pushing them away.

As I got older, my anger grew. When my father got drunk, his verbal abuse was relentless. He would put us down until we were mentally beaten into submission. One night he started to abuse my mother verbally. I lost my temper. I grabbed the glass of wine he was drinking and threw it at him. I ran out the door knowing that if he caught me my life would end. My best friend and I went to see several movies before returning home. When we drove into the apartment complex, I noticed my father sitting in our screened-in porch with a drink in his hand. He was waiting for me to walk in. My friend said, "If you walk in there, he's going to kill you." I agreed. I spent the next two days at my girlfriend's house. When I finally returned home, he was sober.

The first time I met my wife, it was at a graduation party at my cousin's house. I answered the door and there she was, an attractive girl with beautiful long hair and brown eyes. I was struck by her humility and kindness. She was very different from my family's loud and boisterous ways. We began dating. Not wanting to fall into the same trap as my parents, I tried so hard to avoid voicing any negative feelings about our relationship. I didn't know what healthy anger was so I never let her know how I felt. The warden told me I would lose her love if I expressed those feelings. As a result, I continued to wear the same mask I had worn for my mother since I was a kid. I gave the impression that I could solve all of her problems, that nothing bothered me. I put all my energy into this role. I would never reveal my inner self. I couldn't. The warden made it clear that she would never accept someone as worthless as me.

My inner voice defined intimacy for me as painful and something to avoid at all costs. I had witnessed what happened to my parents when they became vulnerable with each other. As a result, I found it difficult to express my feelings. I felt like I did not deserve to be heard. Eventually, I got the courage to ask this very special woman to marry me. Now I had to figure out how to be a good husband. When I was a child, much of my happiness depended on how happy I could make my mother. At the time, I did not realize that I had a lot of healing to do before I was capable of having a healthy relationship.

Children brought out the best in me. I could not wait to have kids of my own. Whenever I would see a father showing affection to his child it would make me long for the childhood that I never had. I have a brother who is eleven years younger than me. In many ways, I took on the responsibility of parenting him. We would play ball together and watch movies. I tried to guide him as best I could. When I cuddled with him, it gave me such a warm and loving feeling.

My inner voice continued to haunt and remind me how inadequate I was. I told myself I would never abuse my wife in the ways my father abused my mother. On the outside, our relationship appeared wonderful, but on the inside, there was unfinished business. I continued to deny my feelings. The mask I wore allowed me to pretend that everything was fine. I would say "yes" to anything my wife asked, even if I felt like saying "no." For example, if she asked me to go to a movie I didn't want to see, I would say "yes" and end up resenting her. Part of me expected her to know what I really wanted to do without even asking. Of course, she could not read my mind.

Money and My Attempts to Fix the Emptiness Inside

By the time I graduated from college in 1981, my father's compulsions had taken their toll. Due to heavy drinking, he was suffering from panic attacks. These turned out to be a blessing of sorts. His fear of death gave him the motivation to seek help.

I joined my father's business in the garment industry. The first day he told me a man must always be loyal to his business. Wives and family will betray you, but your business will always be there for you. It was a fast-paced environment. We made trim out of the customer's material and affixed it to the garment as fast as we could. Since the trim was the last step in production before it was shipped to the stores, speediness was vital to meeting the customer's deadlines.

To my surprise, my father's seemingly successful business was hanging on by a thread. He admitted his shortcomings had gotten the best of him and that he was not able to run his business anymore. For many years, my father was the best in his industry. Now, the consequences of his drinking and gambling had caught up to him. His business was on the verge of bankruptcy. Not surprisingly, his employees were lazy, arrogant, and uncaring. Being a caretaker and yearning for his approval, the decision to join his business was easy, but to keep the business afloat I had to make drastic changes.

I wasn't given the authority to fire any of his workers, so I sent them home early without pay. I took on all of their work myself. I worked long hours. Eventually, the employees asked to be let go. I hired new employees who were enthusiastic and ambitious team players. To find new clients and get back former clients, I offered free services. I would tell potential customers that the first time I picked up material from them I would turn it into trim and return the finished product at no cost. The key to my success was returning the trim to them in a matter of hours, knowing my competitors could not accomplish this. This allowed me to successfully get my foot in the door and show our customers how fast and efficient we had become.

Miraculously, my father started getting help for his drinking. A transformation took place as he began telling me how proud he was of my accomplishments. He gave me full credit for saving his business. I thought his praise would remedy my problem. I was wrong. Nothing could heal what was broken inside; my real problem—my victim thinking—continued to be fueled by the warden's voice.

Victim Thinking

It was easy to be the victim, especially when things did not go the way I wanted. I wanted the world to revolve around me. When something did not go my way, I sought comfort in being the victim. The long hours and the financial success of the business could not fill the emptiness inside. I still felt alone and unworthy despite having a loving wife, a big house, expensive cars, and all the money I would ever need. I needed something to ease my internal pain. I chose not to drink because it reminded me of the terrible times I had with my father.

Gambling and Attempting to Fix the Emptiness Inside

Gambling appeared to be the solution to all my problems and became my drug of choice. Gambling helped me forget how I felt. Big losses entitled me to special treatment from the bookies. Even when I won, I knew deep inside that it was only a matter of time before I would lose the money. I even told the bookie to hold my winnings knowing he was going to get it back anyway. The reality was, I was not betting to win, but rather to lose. My compulsion created a need to keep increasing the amount of my bets until eventually I would lose everything. As I gambled more, I was losing substantial amounts of money. While I was making a fortune in my business, I was losing two fortunes to gambling. I remember the day I had to give the bookie $20,000. He met me in his brand new Lincoln Continental and gave me a special number to place my bets where the line would never be busy. I remember saying to myself, I just bought him that car and took the money from my own family.

Throughout my addiction, I tried to convince myself that I was a better man than my father. After all, he was an absentee father who was driven by his own selfish obsessions. In reality, I was no better. My mind was always drifting away to the teams I gambled on. Consumed with self-hatred and guilt, I finally told my wife how much money I lost gambling. I owned a few businesses and was able to pay my debts out of one of them without her knowing. Eventually, I depleted our savings account and my wife discovered our bank book. She took the kids, went to stay with her parents, and told me to get help. My son was three years old, and my daughter was a year old. Although my wife had every right to do what she did, I felt abandoned, just like I did as a child. I didn't deserve to be abandoned as a child, but now that I was an adult I had no one to blame but myself.

Initially, I didn't really want to get help for my gambling problem. It was not until later that I finally made an appointment with a therapist. I was trying to control my addiction, but, as with all addictions, I did not have the power to battle it on my own. About two months later the pain of my destructive actions started to outweigh the joy of gambling. I never wanted to see my family walking out the door again. I made the decision to get help, and I needed a plan of action. This new way of thinking came to influence how I would live the rest of my life. The problem was, the warden did not want his voice ignored.

My therapist made it clear that if I did not stop gambling, I would not find happiness. The warden's voice was stronger than the therapist's voice, so I tried gambling one more time. This time I thought that I could control it. I promised myself that I would only bet on football games, because that is what I had the most success with. By the time the season ended, I had slipped into my past behavior and began betting on basketball games, too, even though I had no success betting on basketball. It occurred to me that I wasn't controlling my addiction, but rather my addiction was controlling me.

The Resulting Destructive Behavior

At this point, I realized I wasn't gambling to win; instead, I was gambling to fill a void inside. The most significant part was finally realizing I would never be able to control my gambling addiction again. I could never gamble casually. Gambling had beaten me into submission. I surrendered and accepted defeat. I was soon back with my therapist who suggested I go to Twelve Step recovery programs and join a therapy group where he was a co-facilitator. This was the first time I realized I had to do the actions I was told to do, not necessarily what I wanted to do. Going to my first Twelve Step meeting was terrifying. I sat in the back of the room with an imaginary wall built around me, covered by layers of fear and shame. I permitted no one to get close.

I didn't know then that these people saw right through this wall. They knew what my problem was long before I did. They knew me because they knew themselves. I was suffering from an illness called "uniqueness." I truly believed that no one could ever understand how I felt inside. When I heard others expressing joy and laughter it was ridiculous to me. I asked myself, How could they be happy when their lives were so screwed up? When they hugged each other at the end of a meeting I felt uncomfortable. For months I could not shake a hand, let alone give someone a hug.

Not surprisingly, I made no connections with any of the people at the meetings. Nonetheless, I kept going. After a few months of going to meetings my wife asked why I never received phone calls from other people in group; she knew that this support was an important healing aspect of Twelve Step fellowships. "They were all ass kissers!" I responded. Beneath the exterior mask of false pride I was a shattered person who eventually realized that these people weren't ass kissers at all. We were joined together because of our common feeling of profound pain. Eventually, I realized they loved and accepted me long before I loved or accepted myself. Once I understood this, I began to embrace the program. I finally allowed help into my life.

I discovered the hard way that complete abstinence from my destructive behaviors was essential for my healing. Without it, my self-hate would become overwhelming. I learned that I can't be in the ring all day boxing with my addiction and expect to work on improving my relationships at the same time.

I continued to go to Twelve Step meetings, individual therapy, and group therapy. In meetings, the compulsive gamblers spoke about the huge amounts of money they lost. One elderly man said he lost more than everyone put together. He lost fifty years of his life to his constant working and gambling. He wasn't around for his children as they grew up. He noticed he was absent in all of his children's pictures. His comment stuck with me. While I realized the ways I was hurting others and myself through my actions, I never considered the experiences I missed with my family, experiences I could never get back.

Between group meetings, I began to make phone calls to other group members to encourage them. While doing this therapeutic activity, that inner voice was telling me this was a waste of time. As a result, it became increasingly difficult to pick up the phone to call people. I wrestled between the benefits of being in group and going back to my old habits and ways of thinking. I was actually grieving the loss of my compulsions as if I were grieving the loss of a loved one.

I never did go back to gambling, and I cut down on the hours I worked. On the surface, things appeared better. On the inside it was a different story. I was still ignoring the reasons why I felt so wounded and defective. While I was no longer medicating my feelings with work or gambling, I soon chose another destructive alternative to ease my pain.

Womanizing and Attempting to Fix the Emptiness Inside

One evening after working late, I had a sexual encounter with a married woman who worked for me. After the encounter, I felt ashamed and disgusted over what I had done. I went home that night and scrubbed my body until my skin was raw. How could I do this? I looked in the mirror and said, "I'm my father's son." No matter how hard I tried, I was doing the same thing to my family that my father did to his. I attempted to justify my actions by telling myself that I was different from my father, but my guilt was unbearable. I coached my kids' teams, always did homework with them, and was there when they needed someone to talk to, yet I betrayed them and my wife in the worst way a man can betray his family. The warden was beating me up with his bat, which made me feel even more worthless.

I was setting up my kids to repeat the same dysfunction passed down to me by my father and by his father before him. Despite the shame, I wasn't ready to work on my brokenness, and I had sex again with this same woman. Throughout this madness, there was a miracle occurring with my father. I started to see a change in him. My parents came to our house just to be with their grandchildren. The special attention he gave them was something that I had never witnessed before with him. He had such patience with them. Both my parents watched the same movies with the children over and over again. Their favorite was *The Land Before Time*. I don't know how many sequels were made, but my children wore out the VHS tapes, watching them with my parents.

In addition to his time, my father gave my children encouragement. The longer he remained sober, the more his goodness came out. Watching the love grow between my children and him was amazing. My father was learning to give and accept unconditional love. The only words my father ever uttered to our children were words of encouragement and love.

Years later, following a checkup at the clinic, his blood work came back abnormal. After a battery of tests, they found a malignant tumor in his stomach. Within just six months, the cancer spread throughout his body. I never felt so helpless. I was so self-sufficient that I felt I could fix anything in life if I worked hard enough at it. With my father's condition, I was so powerless. All I could do is watch him wilt away. My father said he had one favor to ask me. He did not want to see his grandchildren to see him after he became extremely ill and near death. As much as I disagreed with him, I honored his request. Before he died, he said his biggest regret was not being able to see his grandchildren grow up.

One night at the hospital, a priest came to give him some spiritual support. As the priest left the room he told my mother that my father was more spiritual than anyone he had ever met. I found this amazing because when I was in second grade, he ridiculed me when I told him about Noah's Ark. He said, "What, are you stupid, how you could believe that stuff?" After hearing the priest's comment, I discovered that he had found spiritual peace after he stopped drinking. That surprised me as I remember this man as somebody who once only worshiped money.

My parents had been divorced and remarried so many times that nobody knew for sure if they were married at this point in time or not. My father's will was dependent on them being married. It turned out that they were not married at the time. We held a somber wedding ceremony in the hospital, while my father was on his deathbed. My father was hooked up to a morphine drip as he held my mother's hands and repeated their vows. All of my brothers and their wives were there.

I visited my father in the hospital every night. One evening he asked me how his dog was doing. We were watching his dog during this time. Every night when the dog went out to do his business, our three-year-old daughter would greet the dog at the door with a wipe in her hand and clean the dog's bottom. My father laughed so hard that he told me to stop because it was starting to hurt inside.

One particular night in the hospital he felt very weak, and he knew he did not have much time left. Although I felt sadness I didn't know how to express my feelings to him. As I was about ready to leave, he said with a weak, tired voice, "Son, about twenty years ago my father was in the hospital dying of lung cancer. I was sitting right beside him as you are seated beside me, and I could never find the courage to tell him I loved him." I was amazed that even in the midst of my father's physical pain, he was able to recognize my pain. As he tried to reach out to me, the warden would not allow me to let my guard down and hug my father and say, "I love you." I was paralyzed by fear and was silent.

My father was riddled with cancer, and he was frail and weak, yet he still had the power of a ten-foot giant. The warden told me, "Run out of this room as fast as you can. Don't be vulnerable in front of him!" I grasped my father's hand. He pulled me closer and began to weep. The only time I saw my father cry was when he was drunk and seeking forgiveness for being abusive. On the outside, I showed no emotion as he wept. I silently left the room with a horrible lump in my throat. At the time, I didn't have the strength to say "no" to the warden and tell my father that I loved him.

As I approached the hospital elevator, the door opened and out came a friend from one of the meetings I attended. He was visiting someone else in the hospital that night. I gave him a big hug. I needed to hold someone I could trust, and this guy miraculously appeared. In time, as I grew spiritually, I recognized that divine intervention had taken place that day in my life. That guy in the elevator was sent to comfort me because I didn't know how to comfort myself. Without him, I might have chosen a very destructive solution to ease my pain. Within the next few days, I told my father that I loved him.

One week later, my father suffered a stroke, and the doctors induced a coma. My mother asked me to come to the hospital as the doctors did not think my father would make it through the night. He took his final breath the instant my brother and I walked into his room. My mother explained to us that he didn't want to die until all his kids were there.

The wake was two days later. At the funeral home, I recognized more than thirty men and women from the groups and Twelve Step meetings I attended. Once they heard about my father's death from my wife, word spread quickly to the other group members. I was touched by their kindness. For the first time I had a sense of belonging and connection that I had been searching for my entire life. The message I received from their presence told me I was important, that I mattered. No amount of money, expensive cars, or houses gave me the feeling of warmth I felt that day from these people.

I was beginning to grow. I had the willingness to seek help, but now I acquired a willingness to *take direction* and do what others suggested I do. I was ready to trust others enough to let my guard down and let them see the parts of me that I had covered up for so long because of my shame. I realized that I subconsciously chose to be unhappy because that was familiar to me, especially when faced with frightening changes. I didn't like to own my character defects, especially when I was exposed to challenges. Eventually I learned that when I own my defects, I can respond to challenges in a much healthier way.

I became willing to take direction and do what I was told to do, regardless of how I felt. I began to surrender control which resulted in huge changes in my life. I began to practice humility and swallow my pride. My priorities changed. My businesses were not as important anymore. I eventually sold the businesses that required me to be there and helped the long-time employees who were faithful to me find employment in the industry. I kept my real estate business enterprises that were run by others. I had the luxury of retiring young.

I needed to learn why I kept going from one false solution to the next. To accomplish this, I spent years going to retreats, workshops, groups, meetings, and therapy. During this time, I stayed away from all of my destructive behaviors and did what I was told to do. I listened to the healers in my life that consisted of my therapist, sponsors in the Twelve Step fellowships, and many of the people I met in groups and meetings. I also listened to the stories of other recovering people who were trying to find hope and peace in their lives.

As I began to better understand myself, I started helping others with similar destructive behaviors. Eventually, I held support groups in my home for a diverse group of people, including rabbis, priests, doctors, lawyers, plumbers, and the unemployed. These groups helped people work directly on healing and growth. Some group members spun off to create their own sub-groups. Over time, the group itself became a valuable tool in the healing process for all. These were not just people with addictions, but others who wanted to explore the reasons they acted in ways that sabotaged their happiness. Some of the group members were mystified why they kept choosing relationships that only brought destruction to their lives.

I learned I would never recover until I accepted and embraced the emotional scars of the past. I needed to face the real problem, instead of smashing someone in the mouth whenever provoked. I was only able to realize the real problem when I finally confessed to feeling broken inside. My problems were never gambling, working, or womanizing. These were poor solutions to my real problem. My real problem was my victim thinking. My childhood wounds created a distorted view of life. The warden's voice kept giving me the faulty information that was fed to me as a child. I finally discovered I could not afford to be imprisoned by the warden for the rest of my life. I became more comfortable trusting other people. As my self-esteem improved, I no longer needed the validation from others to feel worthy. I started to *listen* to the people who directed my growth, rather than *fight* them.

If I managed my business like I managed my life, I would have gone bankrupt. I may even have fired myself. When I stepped down from the position of managing my life and took direction from others, my growth accelerated.

As my father found peace during the last ten years of his life, baking became his hobby. He taught my young children how to bake. His specialty was cream puffs, which were so heavy they required a shovel rather than a spoon. He compiled a cookbook consisting of his best calorie-laden desserts.

My mother gave the cookbook to my wife after my father died. One afternoon as I began to look through the cookbook, I discovered that it included more than just recipes. In fact, every other page contained my father's journaling. He wrote down all of his fears, pains, and feelings each day. Since I was struggling with my feelings at the time, I was overcome with emotion. I always viewed my father as a ten-foot giant who could handle anything. I never saw him show fear. He took charge of every situation. For the first time, my father appeared the same size as others. He was not the indestructible and heartless person I knew as a child, but rather someone in pain and in need of help. He was just a flawed human being like all the rest of us. My father reminded me of myself. His journal and mine were similar in that we both disclosed the pain that we hid behind a mask. Like father, like son. We lived with shame and the fear of God and others. Like me, my father had learned to trust others, and this helped heal his pain.

After I read the journal entries, I made an appointment with my therapist. When I arrived, I uncharacteristically burst into tears. What I read in those journal entries had touched something deep inside of me. For the first time, I saw my father with no mask, no toughness, and no perfection. He had stripped himself down to bare skin and bones. He was human, after all. Only then, when reading my father's innermost thoughts and feelings, did I permit myself to find a deeper forgiveness for myself and for him.

The Power of an Inner Voice

That inner voice, the warden, knew my vulnerability. Through my written inventories I discovered one of the many false messages he told me was that asking for help was a sign of weakness. He kept me away from the help I needed to heal. I struggled so long to find forgiveness and a spiritual connection. When I got down on my knees to pray, I felt paralyzed with shame and fear. The warden made it clear that I didn't deserve the love of anyone, including God.

My mother was imprisoned by her warden as well. She regrets her actions just as I did mine. My father's insanity created some of the insanity within my mother. Raising four children while dealing with my father's behaviors was not easy. My mother lived in constant fear, never knowing my father's whereabouts or when the next bomb would go off. Even with this chaos, my mother tried to hold things together as best as she could. She also made holidays and birthdays as special as possible. These are the memories that bring warmth to me, memories I'm happy to share with my children. My mother was nineteen when I was born, so in many ways she was a child herself. She, too, was hurting inside and looked for me to give her what she could not get from my father. Her fear of losing him sent her into self-survival. She was like a drowning person who would pull anyone down in her need to get air.

My mother's father was a very kind and gentle man, but he was also an alcoholic, and alcoholism leaves emotional scars on loved ones. All of us from discouraged childhoods have our own warden, just as my mother did. If my mother could have found a support group, she might have allowed others to carry her through those difficult times when she felt so alone. She didn't understand how her actions affected others. I also find it difficult, at times, to believe I was capable of doing what I did to those I loved the most. Today my mother is still a wonderful source of love and support for our children.

I Am My Father's Son

I remember the night I looked in the mirror, with rage, and said, "I am my father's son." All of the hatred I felt spewed out toward my father. I also recall hating myself for bringing the same wreckage into my home that my father brought into his. Today, my feelings for my father emanate from the loving messages he gave my children and the love he received from people he helped. I am proud to be my father's son. Today when I watch a movie or television show about a father and son relationship, it brings up deep feelings of emotion. As a boy, I so desperately wanted to feel loved and special.

By the time my father found peace, I was still dealing with my own demons. Because he died at age fifty-seven, we missed having quality time together. His death motivated me to make certain that my own children know how much I love them. With my self-acceptance came empathy and compassion for my father. None of this would have been possible had I not taken the steps to heal my internal wounds first.

Complete forgiveness is an ongoing process, beginning with the willingness to take the action of forgiveness rather than choosing the path of victimhood. My father did not hurt me because of something I did. Instead, his actions were a result of his internal demons. He never meant to hurt me, just as I never intended to hurt the people who mattered most to me.

Gratitude and Acceptance

I feel the most grateful at the end of the day when I crawl into bed. There was a time when I dreaded waking up because of how shameful I felt. Today, I finally have peace and appreciate the gift of life. My wife and I enjoy newfound intimacy and I revel in the joys of family life. I feel great joy listening to my youngest son tell me and my wife stories about the world from a perspective of a nine-year-old child. My children share stories about their lives with my wife and I that neither of us could imagine sharing with our parents. This brings us comfort in the knowledge that they trust us this much. Life has its imperfections just as people have their flaws. Most of the time my faith outweighs my fears, but every now and then I slip up and allow the warden's voice to get a little too loud. Usually this happens when I feel entitled or expect the entire world to revolve around me. This is exemplified in my overbearing moments when I tell my wife what she should or should not do, even though she just needs me to be there for her and to listen.

Today, when I hear the warden's voice, I thank him for sharing his opinion, then I redirect my thinking toward healthy actions. These actions may only consist of making a phone call and sharing my thoughts and feelings with those whom I most trust. They continue to hold my hand until I accept myself and remove the mask that shields me from the outside world. Today, I proudly stand as a man without a mask, allowing the world to view me as I am—imperfect, with all my strengths and weaknesses. By removing the mask, I could reach out to others and help them find their way along the journey of life. The ability to help others is a wonderful gift, both for the giver and the recipient.

I found inspiration in Rick Warren's book, *The Purpose Driven Life*. Warren postulates that God will lead you to your true calling in life through the people you trust the most. This gave me pause to reflect. My true calling was in helping others. People began to suggest that I write a book about my life and the healing process that helped me and helped others. My internal voice told me this was too big a task, so I thought I would get more advice. As in the past, I gained courage through the support of others. They gave me the strength to do things I could not have accomplished alone. An example is this book.

After writing an early draft of *The Problem Was Me,* I found myself in uncharted waters. I was wondering how to write it. That is when my path crossed with Abraham Twerski, M.D. A mutual friend introduced us. The idea of asking for help made me uncomfortable. Dr. Twerski put me immediately at ease. He believes that in the core of every human being there is a nucleus of self-respect and dignity.

As I sat in Dr. Twerski's living room, he told me in a gentle, soft-spoken voice about an ex-convict named Avi. He shared, "Some years ago, I began a modest rehabilitation program in Israel for ex-convicts incarcerated for drug-related crimes. During a session with the first group of clients, I illustrated the power of man's natural resistance in the avoidance of damaging some object of beauty. Since everyone knows that drugs are damaging, greater resistance should have been self-enforced before the addiction took hold. But, their lack of resistance was the result of a poor sense of self-worth and the inability to find beauty within their being. Long-term recovery depends on the development of self-esteem, and when healing begins the urge to inflict self pain is diminished."

Avi, one of the ex-convicts, asked, "How can you expect me to have self-esteem? I am thirty-four years old, and sixteen of those thirty-four years have been spent in prison. When I'm released from the penitentiary, who will hire me? When the social worker tells my family that I'll be released in ninety days, nobody is happy. I am a burden and an embarrassment to everyone in the family, and I'm sure they would rather I stay locked up forever until the day I die. How am I supposed to get self-esteem?"

Dr. Twerski's response was, "Avi, have you ever seen a display of diamonds in a jewelry store window? Those diamonds are scintillatingly beautiful and worth hundreds of thousands of dollars. Do you know what they looked like when they first were brought out from the diamond mine? They were ugly, dirty pieces of glass that anyone would think worthless.

"At the diamond mine, there is an expert called a maven who scrutinizes the ore. He may pick up a dirty piece of glass while marveling at the precious gem that lies within. After he sends it to the processing plant, it emerges as the magnificent and brilliantly shining diamond that you view at the jeweler.

"No one can place anything of beauty into a dirty piece of glass. The beauty of the diamond was always present, but it was concealed by layers of material that had long camouflaged its original exquisiteness. The processing plant only removed these layers of grime to reveal its natural beauty; it did not create the beautiful stone.

"I may not be a maven on diamonds, but I am a maven on people. You have a beautiful soul that has been covered with layers of ugly behavior. Therapy will help to rid yourself of all those years of ugliness and reveal the natural beauty of your human soul."

Avi remained in the program for several months before being

transferred to a transitional facility for another eight months. When he finally was released, he obtained a job and remained drug free.

One day Annette, the administrator of the AA program, received a call from a family whose elderly mother had died, leaving an apartment full of useless furniture. They offered to donate the furniture to the rehabilitation program. Annette telephoned Avi and asked him to help move the furniture. Avi reassured her that he would get a truck to move the furniture.

Two days later, Avi phoned Annette back to inform her that he was at the apartment, but there is no point in moving the furniture as it was old and dilapidated. Annette, who did not want to disappoint the family, asked that the furniture be brought to the office in hopes that perhaps someone could restore some of it.

Avi loaded the truck and delivered the furniture to the facility, located on the second floor of the building. As he dragged the old sofa up the stairs, an envelope fell out from beneath the cushions. That envelope contained five-hundred shekels ($1,800 in American currency). This was found money that nobody knew existed, and the rule of "finders-keepers" could easily have been applied, especially by someone like Avi who used to break into houses for a mere ten shekels.

Instead, Avi called Annette and told her about the money. "That's the family's money," she said. "Call them and tell them." When the family heard the story, they donated the five-hundred shekels to the rehabilitation program.

When Annette relayed the story to Dr. Twerski, he turned to Avi and said, "Do you remember our first meeting when you did not know how you could ever obtain self-esteem? It was then that I told you about your inner soul, that beautiful diamond that was buried within you. Many people who never stole a penny in their life may simply have pocketed that money. Not you. What you did was exceptional and revealed the true beauty of the diamond that is your soul."

Some months later, Avi affixed a bronze plaque on the door of the Rehabilitation Center that read: "DIAMOND PROCESSING CENTER." This is why I began to help others because of my love of exposing beautiful diamonds.

As I left Dr. Twerski, I thought about my father. Both of us were dirty pieces of glass with precious gems inside, deeply hidden from view. Once the dirt was washed away, we were freed from fear. Our goodness, the diamonds inside, could finally be revealed. During our conversation, Dr. Twerski agreed to help with my book. As I share my life story, he shares what he's learned as a psychiatrist in the field of addiction. Together, we aspire to help free you and other people from the destructive roles we play in our lives.

Chapter Three: Enter the Warden

If the messages given by the child's caregiver
do not match the actions they show, then distrust, fear,
and confusion permeate the child's belief system.

೮೨೦೧೩

I self-medicated with work, gambling, and womanizing to ease the pain of my perceived failures. Whether gambling, drinking, overeating, pornography, over-spending, or compulsive cleaning, the culprit is usually a flawed belief system that propels people from one harmful behavior to another, or from one bad relationship to another.

Dr. Twerski explained to me how early life experiences affect our lives. Dr. Twerski says, "We walk in the same way we did when we took our first steps. Much of our automatic behavior is derived from early life lessons. When we attempt to change these behaviors, we meet strong resistance. We enter the world as helpless creatures and are totally dependent on our parents for our very survival. As children grow and develop into mature adults it is normal for them to gradually wean themselves from their lifeline of support, the parents who nurtured them from birth. But, the child who grew in body, but whose spirit remains scarred from childhood, will not be able to successfully shed his apron strings. These children have difficulty adjusting to reality and lapse into some form of addictive behavior. Until, of course, they seek help for their problems.

"When a group of psychologists jointly constructed an experimental house for adults, proportioned according to the size that a normal house would feel like to a small child, the ceilings were thirty feet high and the adults were forced to stand on their toes to reach the chairs and tables. All doorknobs were out of their reach. When a control group of normal adults inhabited the house, they began to exhibit neurotic symptoms within only two days. But, this is reality for our small children who feel dwarfed by the large world in which we live. Without parents to serve as intermediaries, life for our children would be intolerable."

Messages that Drive Our Behavior

A core belief system is the network of messages that tell us what to do to survive. It also forms the basis of our attitudes and perceptions so we know who and what to fear and trust, and what we should expect from others. It is based on the early influences of family, teachers, and peers. A faulty belief system makes it difficult to perceive the world in realistic terms and keeps our fears at bay. Healthy information from outside sources helps provide stability and comfort in the face of helplessness, hopelessness, and despair.

Children have a distorted perception of the world. If their father removes a splinter from their mother's finger and she says, "Ouch," they may think their father is harming their mother by inflicting pain. If a sibling is ill and their parents spend extra time caring for their sick child, the brother or sister may come to the conclusion, "They love him more than me."

My biggest misconception was the way I perceived how others saw me. Since I viewed myself as defective, my assumption was that others saw me that way. This is why I shielded myself from vulnerable situations. When I was a child, being vulnerable brought pain and misery. I chose to avoid intimacy, believing if I let down my guard, even with my wife, I might be wounded in the same way my parents hurt me. The consequences of not being intimate were staggering. In addition to being a victim, I was filled with profound loneliness. I believed that I was entitled to harmful behaviors because they ultimately brought me comfort. This resulted in me being angry with myself and everyone else. It was as if everyone was out to get me. I blamed everybody . . . except myself.

I believed I was the center of the universe and the world owed me everything I didn't receive as a child. The real problem was my fear of vulnerability and my tendency to not allow anyone close enough to be intimate. I created unrealistic expectations of people when they didn't give me what I wanted. I was, after all, "the victim."

My behavior in many ways mirrored that of an adolescent, which is where my emotional growth stopped. My sense of entitlement created the basis for my distorted thinking. I turned my attention to the shortcomings of others as a way to focus away from myself and to escape my own pain and misery. To feel better, I relied on my addictions.

Vicious Cycle of Pain

Fears

addiction and/or imprisonment of childhood wounds.

victim thinking

isolation, loneliness

delusions
(I'm not the problem; it's everyone else who needs help.)

self-righteousness, self-pity

acting out or acting in

If you do not reprogram your belief system, you will continue to choose one bad solution after another. Although people may be aware of their own destructive belief systems, it is hard to break old patterns and shut off old voices. The longer these messages have been playing in your life, the more difficult it is to turn them off. To make changes, you need to be aware of your faulty belief system. It will help you heal and grow. Then, you need to take action. This won't be easy. Old voices can loudly tell us that we can't trust anything we can't control. Finding a support group where you feel comfortable will help you deal with old wounds that resurface.

Dr. Twerski believes that we live and act according to our sense of perceptions. According to Dr. Twerski, "When we see something, we generally do not think we are viewing some optical illusion. Travelers in the desert are known to observe the occasional mirage, such as an optical illusion of water ahead. On close inspection, the water does not exist. In our daily lives, mirages do not exist. On the other hand, our eyes may not fail us, but the information we receive through our senses is processed by our mind and may undergo distortion. For example, it is not unusual for an adult to panic at the sight of a small, harmless puppy. This may stem from some fear experienced in childhood when the child was frightened by a dog that barked and jumped on him. Our subconscious mind may not mature with time. From the vantage point of an adult, our subconscious views the harmless puppy as a huge, ferocious dog. As anyone who has dealt with dog phobias knows, the logical explanation that this is a harmless puppy is to no avail. Panic supersedes reason. Impressions that reside in the subconscious mind may overwhelm logical thought and cause us to respond according to our subconscious impression rather than to any factual reality."

When my life became unmanageable, I tried anything and everything to bring about change. No matter what I did, I felt broken inside. Although I intended to seek help, I did nothing until I made the conscious decision to do so. I had good intentions, but, ultimately, actions are all that count. I needed something to give me the necessary catalyst to change. Weekly therapy sessions and workshops helped me understand what had happened during my childhood to cause me to seek such harmful solutions. In addition to that, I also needed daily disciplines to transform my attitudes about life and people. These disciplines came in the form of daily connections with the people in my therapy groups and meetings. These were the people I trusted most.

To help heal my wounds, I needed to take two different kinds of inventories. One inventory showed how my parents and teachers influenced my concept of what an authority figure represented to me as an adult. If I did not trust my parents to care for me as a child, it's not surprising that I found it difficult to trust others. My early relationship with my father also affected many of the relationships I had with authority figures, including supervisors, sponsors, spouses, and even spiritual leaders. It took some time to develop new positive inner voices to substitute negative messages I received as a child. Today, I am grateful for the many people who have helped to reinforce the positive messages while providing support when my thinking goes haywire.

The second inventory dealt with childhood wounds. I began to realize how thoughts of worthlessness and defectiveness affected my relationships with other people. I learned how easily childhood wounds could be reopened when I became agitated or someone struck a raw nerve. When I felt pain, I either shut down in shame or lashed out in anger. Through therapy, I discovered it's not my choice that painful events occur, but I do have a choice in how I handle those events. I can either seek help from my support group or permit myself to become a victim. Written inventories are discussed in more detail in Chapter Eight. Pages 99 and 111 have useful examples of how to do inventories. Appendix A on pages 151 and 152 also contains blank inventories for readers to photocopy and use for pesonal use.

My belief system has changed for the better. Instead of misery and turmoil, I am more serene, accepting, and self-forgiving. Whatever overwhelmed me in the past now lacks the same power. During this journey, I discovered a new voice that told me that I no longer had to carry the load of others. This does not mean that my old beliefs went away. I still hear echoes from the past and need to be mindful at all times.

The diagram on the following page, shows how our belief system can be corrupted by childhood wounds, leading to self-destructive behaviors. This allows your inner voice to take control of your actions. Note that the diagram does not take into account other factors, including mental health disorders or compromised social environments. Living in poverty or other oppressive situations affects shame levels and self-esteem.

The Old Belief System

Guided by Wounds and Destructive Messages

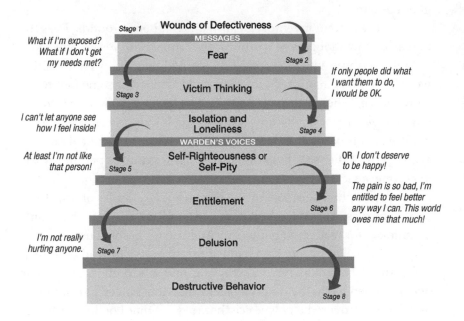

Stage One: Wounds of Defectiveness

Defectiveness begins from the earliest messages we receive as children from parents and guardians. Healthy messages tell children that they are loved unconditionally. Unhealthy messages tell them that something is wrong with them. When authority figures don't feel good about themselves, it becomes difficult for them to model self-esteem to children. Since children don't have the ability to understand these complicated dynamics, they blame themselves for the defects and shortcoming of their guardians. Over time, they develop coping mechanisms and begin to adopt the faulty belief system as their reality. When they mature, their inner voice tells them to hide their true self from the world.

Stage Two: Fear

Healthy fears protect us from harm. On the other hand, manufactured fears can be harmful and insulate us from experiencing joy. The stories I create in my head initiate a process I refer to as *awfulization*. This is a process where my belief system plays out the end of the story to an awful conclusion. People with untreated emotional wounds have greater fears than those who grew up in healthy environments. Since they have often experienced disappointment in the past, they expect and fear not having their needs met in the future. Past emotional depravation prepares them to expect the same in the future.

Stage Three: Victim Thinking

When children are victimized, they carry victim thinking into their adult lives. They expect others to fill their existing emptiness. For example, if a child grew up hungry, the fear of hunger may perpetuate well into adulthood, even if the person has plenty of food available. The same occurs if a child grew up without enough nurturing. The child seeks more nurturing in her adult life and expects more from those around her. When someone needs more than others can give, it is a prescription for disaster.

Stage Four: Isolation and Loneliness

Inner voices tell us to isolate ourselves to deal with a world that will not accept us. As a result, we don't share our thoughts with others, increasing the likelihood that our thinking will become distorted. We believe that trusting others will only be harmful and we'll be harshly judged. Instead, we connect with our inner voice.

Stage Five: Self-righteousness or Self-pity

Looking at ourselves eventually becomes so painful that we focus on the shortcoming of others instead. We make a decision to be either self-righteous or wallow in self-pity. We don't like to connect with others, unless it's with the wrong people. The warden justifies our distortions.

Stage Six: Entitlement

When the pain inside becomes more intense, the person either acts inward, outward, or both. Acting in can occur when we internally berate ourselves for the mistakes we make. Acting out can occur when we engage in destructive behaviors that are obvious to others, as with addictions. The self-righteous person feels entitled to behave destructively, regardless of the harm he or she causes. Essentially, they give themselves permission to act out in destructive ways.

Stage Seven: Delusion

Eventually, the combination of manufactured fears and victim thinking makes all thoughts and stories real. Isolation convinces us that we are right as we settle into our comfort zone as victims. Focusing on the shortcomings of others becomes more natural than looking within. This faulty belief system supports our position that the world is the problem, not us. As time goes on, the pain intensifies.

Stage Eight: Destructive Behaviors

All belief system stages are built on the foundation of negative core beliefs, which were developed from childhood wounds. The cycle starts over again in stage one, when the person is triggered by someone or something that recreates the feeling of defectiveness.

Chapter Four: Intrusive Messages

*Eventually we learn it is all right to say "no," and
we recognize how we had empowered fears to control our life.
The more we do this, the more we learn that our fears
are more imagined than real.*

෧෨

Reaching back to the messages we heard in childhood will help us discover what needs to be healed. Only by admitting that our best thinking is not working can we work toward finding a cure. Some people need to experience something catastrophic before attempting to improve their situation. Many of us continue through life until we fall off a cliff, arriving at a state of complete hopelessness and despair.

Earlier, Dr. Twerski told the story of Avi, an ex-convict, who was nearing the end of his incarceration only to be told by family members that they were unhappy about his impending freedom. They gave him the message that he was a burden and an embarrassment. It was their right to feel this way. Unfortunately for him, not only was he physically incarcerated most of his life, but mentally imprisoned by his feelings of total worthlessness. His sentence began long before he was locked up. He remained powerless to change until he became aware of how the intrusive messages from early childhood led him to a lifetime of ugly behavior. Before he could find peace, he had to control his addictive behavior. Only then could he begin a journey back in time where he would discover the meaning of those early messages that held him hostage.

Why do we turn to actions that will only create more problems for ourselves and others when we are in despair? Why do we allow ourselves to be deceived into thinking these actions will make us feel better, even though they cause nothing but grief, guilt, and self-loathing? It is insane to believe the lie that, "Next time will be different." If someone lied to you repeatedly, you would stop trusting that person. Yet, those of us with intrusive childhood messages continue to believe the lies. We are delusional, incapable of important decision making, and crippled by our dysfunctional state of mind. Figuring all of this out is like putting together pieces of a puzzle.

Puzzling Behavior

The first piece of the puzzle is to discover how we became the person we are today. We are all products of messages handed down from parents, teachers, friends—even the media. Nobody is born a bad person. We are the product of our experiences and our environment. If we can accept the reality of our situation, we can rid ourselves of self-loathing. The second piece of the puzzle is to understand how early intrusive messages may have formed the basis of our belief system. Negative internal voices can unleash a tsunami of destructive thinking that interferes with our ability to think clearly and enjoy healthy relationships.

In attempting to understand more about our belief system, old information and new information are significant. New information is the healthy set of messages we receive from our therapists and support groups. Conversely, old information is the messages we received in childhood that formed the basis of our dysfunctional families.

The Power of Authority Figures

One of the most powerful messages I ever received came from my nine-year-old son. While watching a baseball game on television, my son asked me why the kids in the stands were so excited. I said some baseball players are heroes to those kids. I suggested that some day one of those players might be his hero. My son paused and said to me, "They may be my hero someday, but you will always be my first hero." I was so touched, I could not reply. As parents we are our children's first heroes, whether we want the responsibility or not.

As children, our parents or adult caregivers were the dominant authority figures. The messages they communicated to us, healthy or otherwise, influence our thinking and behavior for the rest of our lives. These messages, which are deeply rooted, tell us how us how others in the world view us. Changing one's belief system requires a willingness to be open minded. People need the equivalent of an anti-virus program for computers to filter out unhealthy, intrusive messages that threaten our lives. If these intrusive messages are not processed by a healthy support system, they can create destructive actions. The greater the pain, the more intense the fear and the louder the demands of the warden's voice.

Normal and Irrational Fear

Fear is normal and often necessary to protect us from danger. Healthy fear alerts us to danger. For example, with healthy fear we look twice before crossing the street. On the other hand, irrational fear paralyzes us, and we become incapable of taking that first step toward freedom. If we become too afraid to even cross the street, we may never know the joys that wait on the other side. Other people have no fears at all. They carelessly dash into dangerous situations. The solution is to find a healthy, balanced perspective toward our fears. A therapist or support group can serve as your guiding force to help you face these situations and arrive safely at your destination. As we discover more about ourselves, we may find that many of our fears originate from within and have no basis in reality. When I finally found the courage to face my fears, to tune out my inner voice, and to ask for help, I began my journey toward acceptance and understanding. Otherwise, I might never have been able to experience the joy and serenity of a balanced and fruitful life.

When a child lives in constant fear, the child's view of the world becomes distorted. Fear is a great motivator to succeed, but it also can be deceiving if what's really driving us is the fear of failure. We feel defective inside, and one of the ways we protect this secret is by hiding behind a mask. The fear of never being good enough can drive a person toward achieving financial success under the faulty assumption that it will fix the defective feeling inside. If the pursuit of success is merely to cover up feelings of inadequacy, then only the symptoms are treated and not the actual wound that caused the insecurity. It took me some time before I recognized that this was exactly what I was doing to hide my low self-esteem.

Toxic Shame

If we do not feel good about ourselves, we don't want others to get too close. Toxic shame, along with fear, separates us from our family and the rest of the human race. Toxic shame informs us that we are to blame for the problems of our parents and for everything else that goes wrong in our lives. The burden of carrying all this shame damages our self-esteem. Excessive shame takes our rights away. We give up the right to say how we feel, the right to express anger, and even the right to be loved. It distorts our processing and causes us to overreact because we take everything as a deliberate act of disrespect toward us. Whenever I was criticized I took it as a personal indictment. I allowed the criticism and the resulting shame to define me as a person. If my wife brought up any of my shortcomings, I would overreact and immediately become defensive. Also, when people's behavior does not match their values it creates a tremendous amount of shame. I never wanted to behave the way my father did. When I began acting like him, the shame this created was unbearable.

Shame is also the toxic fuel that drives destructive behaviors. It brings us to the doorstep of addiction and invites us in so we forget who we are and how hopeless we have become. We are deluded into thinking that certain actions will make us happy and ease our pain. When my wife brought up the impact of my indiscretions on her and our children, it touched the deepest core of my shame. The feeling of worthlessness and pain brought me to a new level of hopelessness. I would either shut down emotionally or fly into a rage. The anger was directed at my wife, but caused by shame I felt deep inside.

Lack of Trust

It is normal for young children to think only of themselves. When my son was five years old he asked me what present I was going to get him for Father's Day. We enter this world dependent on the nurturing and unconditional love of our parents or guardians. We expect them to take care of us and speak the truth. Trust breaks down as we begin to notice the differences between what they say and what they do. For me, as a child, I received the message that I was an object to be used for the benefit of fulfilling the needs of my parents. My mother said that she loved us kids more than anything or anyone in this world, yet her actions elicited a different impression.

Sometimes as children we may have felt invisible, as if our feelings did not matter. Sometimes the messages we received about love did not reflect the actions we witnessed. This discrepancy can create a destructive inner voice that warns us about the pain we will receive if we trust others later in life. Our inability to trust directly influences our ability to experience intimacy. In the end, all of our relationships are negatively affected.

Perfectionism as a Way of Life

Perfectionism is doomed to failure because no one is perfect. To err is human, and we all are members of the same flawed human race. But, when we focus on our shortcomings rather than celebrating the things we do right, it creates unrealistic expectations for ourselves and for others. It also sets us up to be the victim because we believe others judge us the way we judge ourselves. A perfectionist must have everything just right or life is viewed as a failure. There is no gray area. Perfectionism also blocks us from trying new things because we don't want to fail or be considered a failure. We become hard on ourselves and judge others. We ask, "Why should I have tolerance for people if they have none for me?" I never viewed mistakes as a normal part of life. Instead, I saw failure as an unforgivable and unbearably shameful thing.

Perfectionism makes it difficult to accept opinions from others. Our inner voice tells us we are defective if someone disagrees with us. My wife once said that she could not discuss certain issues with me because I always needed to be right. My mask of perfection hid my shame. For me being wrong was too much to bear. What never occurred to me was that others accepted me for myself although I could not. Pete's story demonstrates the pitfalls of perfectionism.

Pete

Pete is a married man in his forties. He is a successful
professional who is highly respected in his field. According to Pete,
"As a child growing up in a household where both parents were active
alcoholics, trauma was a daily event. One such event occurred when
my father, amidst one of his drunken rages, told me I was a mistake
and should have never been born. I was devastated. As a result, I spent
a lot of time trying to prove this wasn't so. I decided to excel in all
aspects of my life to prove to them that I was no mistake. Long after
my friends went home from school to be with their families, I often
stayed in the schoolyard. I fantasized about making the winning basket
while shooting hoops, pitching the last inning of the World Series as
I threw a ball against a brick wall, or scoring the winning touchdown
during the Super Bowl while kicking a ball in the air.

"In this fantasy world, I was the star and not the mistake.
When I finally got into organized sports, I wanted to show others that
I mattered. I played Pop Warner football at age seven. The father of
one of my friends was the head coach and probably knew the story of
my home life. As a result, he bought me spikes and helped pay for my
uniform so I could play. I was the smallest player on the team, but with
a no-quit attitude, I became the starting running back. Since the first
game was to take place a block from my house, I was excited knowing
that my parents could easily walk over to watch. The first time that I
carried the ball I ran for a thirty-yard touchdown. I floated on air for
the last five yards because I felt so happy. When I reached the end
zone, I looked for my parents on the sidelines but could not find them.
Later in the game, I ran for a seventy-yard touchdown. By that time,
most of the euphoria had worn off when I realized that my parents
were not there. Even though everyone was cheering, I felt crushed.

"When I went home I found both of them passed out drunk.
I guess I was really a mistake after all. After this, I became even more
determined to succeed. I thought, when they discover how great I am,
they definitely will come watch me. To make sure that I could continue
playing, I worked especially hard during the team fundraising drive.
My friend and I would stand at the local Shop Rite for hours each
Saturday and Sunday to collect donations. We raised the most money

of anyone on the team. When I got home, I put the container in a kitchen cabinet so I wouldn't lose it. The week before I needed to turn in my money, I went to look for the container but it was gone. I could not find it anywhere. My parents told me that the coach would understand if I told him I lost the container full of money. I was frustrated because I didn't lose it. I didn't realize until later that my parents had taken the money to buy booze. When it was time for the meeting, my parents forced me to go and admit to losing the money. The coach was very angry and told me that unless I came up with some money, I couldn't play the next season. My mother told me I couldn't play because they couldn't afford to pay for spikes or the uniform.

"I continue to tell myself that failure is not an option for me and still have the need to prove that I am not a mistake. However, it's impossible to hold myself to such unrealistic expectations. Therefore, whenever anyone, especially my wife, says or insinuates anything that implies weakness or failure, I get extremely angry because it reinforces my childhood feelings of rejection. I had to continue to be perfect because I mattered. This perfectionist attitude has never allowed me to be real or vulnerable with anyone. I hid my feelings by working all the time."

Pete wanted to be perfect so he could be accepted. Rejection by his parents, his shame, and his fear of abandonment created this intense need for him to be perfect. However, he is finally beginning to realize the insanity of the unrealistic expectations that he placed upon himself. If he wasn't perfect in everything he did, his inner voice called him a failure, took over his belief system, and eventually crushed his self-esteem. Whenever Pete felt challenged by someone, his anger would flair up to protect his inner childhood wounds. Psychological scars from the past can only be healed by sharing the sadness with others in a safe, supporting environment. Over time, Pete has begun to feel safe enough to allow his support group to enter a part of his life that had been sealed off. He is now able to share what was once too painful to expose to the outside world. As Pete continued to work on his written inventories, he began to realize that many of his fears were of his own making.

Control Was Part of Survival

Some of us correctly believed that if we were not in control we were in danger because in families like ours, violence was the norm, not the exception. As a young boy, seated at the top of the stairs, I kept a nightly vigil to protect my mother in the event my father came home drunk. This control was, in my belief system, essential because I believed there could be harsh consequences. Control and survival went hand in hand. My inner voice told me that to survive childhood, I needed to take control of the situation. If my father was drunk, I had to be there to protect my mother so she did not get hurt. I also tried to find ways to get my father to come home at night so my mother would be happy. But control, like perfectionism, is a no-win situation and everything eventually spirals out of control. Although an unrealistic way to cope, the need to take charge of everyone is a comfortable role for some of us to play. Controlling impulses are not conducive to maintaining healthy adult relationships. Nobody wants someone else telling them what to do. As long as we expect people to act and think the way we want them to, we are setting ourselves up for major disappointment.

We also have inner controls that stop us from expressing feelings toward others since we *feel* we don't have the right to be heard. Expressing feelings in a healthy way, even in conflict, is an important part of the healing and growth process.

Caretaking

Caretakers put the needs of others before their own. My inner voice tried to reinforce my belief that a good son takes care of his mother's needs before his own. Whenever I put my needs ahead of others, I felt ashamed. The consequences of being my mother's caretaker as a child had harmful effects later in my life. Children who become caretakers find it difficult to ask for help and have an even harder time saying no or being intimate. Caretakers can give the impression of being able to care for everyone and everything, but eventually if they don't ask for help, they break down. Letting go is difficult. They may be self-reliant and dependable, but the irony is, the role they play inhibits them from getting what they really need. As a child and later as an adult, I longed to have someone care for me, but as a caretaker it was more natural to place the needs of others first. Not until I found the courage to invite others into my life and to ask for help was I able to change my attitude and tell the little voice in my head to shut up.

Sara

Sara is a classic caretaker. She blamed herself for all of her family's problems. Sara's fear of confrontation made it impossible for her to let go. Her fear pushed her further into shame and isolation.

According to Sara, "My parents gave me all the material things I needed. There was never physical abuse. On the outside everything appeared fine. My mother never complained. Since she believed that good people don't complain, I wanted to be considered a good person and didn't complain. As a child, I felt our neighbors took advantage of my parents. They came over uninvited and stayed for dinner but never reciprocated. They borrowed items and never returned them. But, my mother never complained and seemed to always keep everything bottled up inside.

"My father was a kind man, but lacked self-esteem and seemed disappointed in me whenever anything went wrong. If a problem developed between me and someone else, my father faulted me, no matter what the circumstances were.

"As an adult, I felt responsible for anything negative that happened in the lives of my husband and children. It was always my fault. When a problem occurred in our household, I was blamed and I'd convince myself that they were right. One evening I received a phone call from my son. He was screaming at me because his car broke down. It was my fault, he implied, so I should immediately pick him up. When my husband learned about my son's car, he shouted at me too. I don't recall the exact words, but the message was clear. Had I gotten the car fixed this would never have happened. As always, I accepted the blame.

"Resentment for my family and myself was growing, but I didn't realize it until it was brought to my attention during a therapy session. Once I started to express my feelings all that pent up anger spewed out from inside of me. I found myself talking faster and faster until I realized that all this baggage had piled up inside of me after years of carrying everyone else's burdens.

"After realizing this lesson, I took the giant step of dealing with my family. I needed to confront them and tell them that I would not put up with their nonsense any longer. In the past, my husband blamed me for everything. I accepted the blame. I apologized when I should not have since I believed that good people didn't complain. Now things are different. Through my support group, I have found the courage to confront my family. I am no longer responsible for everything around the house. As I draw strength from others, I feel a greater sense of self-respect as well as the respect I notice from others. My life today is so much freer than ever before."

With the help of her support group, Sara has begun to realize that she can neither right a wrong, nor can she continue to help those people closest to her without inflicting further harm on herself. Only when she was willing to accept the aid of her support group, could she stand up for herself and ignore the faulty messages generated by her old belief system. Now she realizes that even though she may disagree and argue with a family member, she would never lose their love. By helping herself, Sara also became a better role model for her husband and children.

Alex

Alex, a psychologist, married with two children, has always had problems with intimacy. Alex views women as mere sexual objects. Alex spends a lot of time surfing the Internet and viewing pornography.

According to Alex, "I grew up in a small apartment in a middle-class Jewish neighborhood in New York. I can honestly say that there is nothing my parents wouldn't have done for me, but my brothers and sister always came first. My parents both worked full-time. There were no great traumas, no abuse, and no addictions. I had a simple, safe, loving, and happy childhood. My parents always told me to be a good boy. The message was to be kind and respectful to others, compassionate, thoughtful, patient, and wait your turn. Don't be mean or angry, selfish, boastful, arrogant, or hurt anyone's feelings. See the good in people and accept them for who they are. It also meant work hard in school, be successful, and make us proud. Growing up, I felt that my needs and feelings were not as important as others. I could not be myself if that upset or hurt you. I could not express myself or do what I wanted, if it caused you discomfort. So, I learned to keep my opinions to myself and to be submissive. I paid close attention to nuances in facial expressions and voices to determine if anyone was upset with me, as if my very survival depended on their approval.

"At a young age, I felt that if I was bad I would hurt my mother. Later in life I transferred those feelings to others. When I hurt anyone it would cause me terrible shame and guilt. Throughout my life, I felt as if I was walking on eggshells. I was saying and doing things only to win approval from my mother or others. I kept my true feelings to myself so others did not have the opportunity to know the real me. The only comfort I found was in continuing to project the safe, people pleasing, neutered 'good boy' identity, whose genuine, deeper, and more conflicted self lay hidden in fear. So many times I wanted to break out of my shell, but I was too afraid to surrender. And, as much as that made me feel safe, I felt lonely, shameful, and weak.

"Through therapy I have learned that my mother's love was conditional, and if I didn't please her then I would risk being emotionally abandoned. Now I realize that I was not afraid of losing her love, but rather of causing her pain or making her suffer. The shame was almost unbearable. As an adult, I no longer want to make that sacrifice. I want to be who I am, to be authentic, and to let the world see the real me.

"My parents were also very smothering and wanted to do everything for me. But, there were times when I needed to do things for myself, to solve my own problems. Because my parents would always come to the rescue, I got the message that I could not take care of myself. So, I stopped asking them for help and kept my problems and concerns to myself. If I didn't talk about my problems, then they couldn't take it away, fix it, critique it, or tell me what to do. As a teenager, others would always come to me for advice, but rarely would

I share my own problems. I wanted them to believe that I had it all together. My parents never talked to me about their problems. I was so over protected that I believed having problems was unusual.

"Today I feel overly anxious when my wife becomes upset with me. There's a voice inside me that insists that it can't be my fault because I'm a 'good boy' who doesn't hurt someone else. Therefore, I wind up blaming her for the problems. But I realize now that I'm wrong to believe she will walk out on me, then leave me alone to face my loneliness if I make a mistake. Maybe people pleasing is a way to avoid my loneliness. Instead, I focus on the feelings of others and how I can please them, rather than concentrating on my own sense of helplessness at not being able to fill up the empty, lonely place inside of me."

Alex's wounds were not as visible as most, but on closer examination, he somehow received the message that his role in life was to be a people pleaser. All of his messages and inner voices suggested that he had to act in a certain way regardless of how he felt. His feelings were dismissed unless they fell into the category of being a good son, a good husband, or a good father. His happiness could only be achieved through the happiness of others. Alex also learned to avoid conflict. He thought he would lose the love of his family if he disagreed with them. So, he accepted full responsibility regardless of whether he owned the problems or not.

Whenever a problem arose with a loved one, the imaginary guy on his shoulder would hit him over the head with a bat, blaming him for everything that happened. His clarity improved as he became more willing to open up to his support group. He recognized the personal harm from his distorted sense of family loyalty. He asked his support group to help him overcome that fear. For instance, he would agree to call me if he had an argument with a family member and was fearful that the conflict would cause separation, abandonment, or rejection. The fear of abandonment can be so terrifying that it can cause some people to say or do anything to make the fear go away. This fear distorted Alex's thinking. As the honest and caring person that he was, Alex frequently made promises he couldn't keep because he didn't want to disappoint or hurt anyone's feelings. This negatively affected his credibility until he could finally accept the truth and look at himself honestly for the first time.

Eventually, Alex would learn that it was OK to say no and that his family would not abandon him for turning them down. Having an addiction to pornography was safe for Alex because he did not have to deal with the expectations that occur in a real life relationship. There are no confrontations or expectations with pornography. Earlier in his life when Alex had relationships with other women they would quickly dissolve before any commitments were made.

Dr. Twerski suggests that problems may arise even without abusive parenting. According to Dr. Twerski, "Children must be disciplined and limitations must be set. A five-year-old child may want ice cream before dinner and is not capable of understanding why he should not have it. All he knows is that someone is refusing something he wants, and he may react with, "I hate you, Mommy." Although most children are not adversely affected by proper discipline, instances may arise when even good discipline elicits a strong negative feeling toward a parent. This can put the child in conflict if he or she feels that hostility directed toward a parent jeopardizes his or her security. The juvenile mind may deal with this conflict in a variety of ways. Realize that some thoughts and feelings that enter children's minds may linger for years and affect their adult behavior.

Distorted Anger

When the support of healthy role models is absent in a child's life, the child who received mixed signals is at a tremendous disadvantage when required to respond to anger. He may either react in rage or shut down altogether. Either way, the child's anger is not processed in a healthy way. Like Alex, if a child is informed that a good boy does not complain and does as he is told, chances are that his internal messages will direct him to stuff the feeling and avoid conflict since he is angry. Eventually, this won't work because a volcano forms inside until it eventually explodes. As a child, I took my anger out on my brothers even though they did nothing to deserve my wrath.

We try to control our sadness by not allowing ourselves to cry. The message is that big boys don't cry because it is a sign of weakness. My father tried to challenge this old belief in the hospital before he passed away. I couldn't cry in front of my father under any circumstance. This message was so ingrained that I couldn't let it go even though he was dying. My inner voice told me to hide my anger in front of my wife and kids because I would remember how angry my parents were with each other, and how I suffered as a result. So fearful was I of bringing anger into my own home that I never asserted myself. As a result, I created a sense of isolation and I would react in anger when something unexpected happened. Anger is controlling and leads to self-righteousness. The feeling of superiority is transient. By focusing on the shortcomings of others rather than our own failures, the result will be feelings of resentment and a victim mentality.

Selfishness

Selfishness, like isolation, is inherent in dysfunctional families. If the child of alcoholic parents can only rely on himself, then selfishness becomes a coping mechanism or survival skill. He quickly learns that nobody can do for him what he can do for himself. Eventually, the child becomes his own higher authority and can never accept trust or guidance from others. This selfish thinking, which was once needed for survival, is carried into our adult life, but naturally it is not popular with others.

Selfishness leads to a very serious character defect known as destructive entitlement. Destructive entitlement and self-pity become a great tag team and when combined can produce destructive actions. Unfortunately, destructive thinking can be very delusional. When the inner voice tells us we can do certain things, it neglects to inform us of the terrible consequences.

I recall the first time I sought outside help. One evening I received a call from my father, who by then had been in recovery for nearly ten years. With a sad voice he said, "Maybe now we can stop the insane thinking before it hits your children." I did not understand the impact of his statement until years later. I also did not want to hand down to my children the negative messages that I grew up with from childhood. I realized that I had to change my belief system so I would not transfer those same sick messages to my children.

Be aware of the ways that belief systems are formed and how childhood wounds affect our perception of life. We cannot change our emotional wounds unless we first find out what is broken. If we never learn what intrusive messages we received in childhood, we cannot pass down healthy messages to our children. These wounds, if untreated, will block any chance of recovery or intimacy, and we will be destined to listen to the commands of our inner voice for the rest of our lives.

Chapter Five: Childhood Wounds

If others were to look beyond our masks,
would they ever accept what is buried deep inside?

ℰℭ

Imagine if you had an open wound. Next, think about your wound being poked at constantly as you go through your day. As you were enduring this, you would most likely find ways to hide this wound to protect yourself from the pain of other people's actions. While emotional wounds aren't as obvious as the physical kind, they can be just as painful.

While driving, when another driver cuts you off, how do you react? Why do we get so angry, even if there was no harm or accident? The amount of negative energy we burn is not proportional to the incident. Where does all this anger come from? Most likely, the other driver doesn't know us, yet we give him or her tremendous power over our emotions because our wound was reopened. The deeper that wound, the greater the control it has over us, and the greater the lengths we go to hide and protect it.

In my experience of helping others, it becomes apparent that for many, everyday experiences such as driving shake up a sense of being dismissed, invisible, inadequate, or worthless. These feelings often stem from untreated childhood events or trauma.

Dr. Twerski refers to a psychological maneuver known as *transference.* According to Dr. Twerski, "A person may transfer feelings that were appropriate toward person A to person B. To the conscious mind, which operates logically, a wheel is just a wheel, not a car, and a sleeve is just a sleeve, not a suit. The subconscious mind operates according to different rules: the part equals the whole. A wheel can be a car, and a sleeve can be a suit."

Have you ever met someone who, at first sight and before

exchanging a single word, you immediately dislike? Conversely, do you recall meeting a person who, upon first sight, you decide, "This is a nice person." Why would you have negative or positive feelings toward someone you've never met before? It is not logical. However, the subconscious mind is not logical.

According to Dr. Twerski, you may have had a grade school teacher (like I did), who was downright mean. Thirty years later I entered an office, and when I first met the secretary I disliked her, although I didn't know why. She reminded me of my fifth grade teacher. Although there was just one small similarity to my teacher, the subconscious mind equated the secretary with my teacher. This is what is meant by transference. One transfers the feeling from one person to another or from one object to another.

In situations of transference, our wound may be exposed. As we start to feel diminished or inadequate, our anger swells to cover the pain of the wound. When this happens, the guy on our shoulder with a bat thinks only about protecting our tender emotional wound and not about the other person's point of view. Meanwhile, we create distance from others. Over time this becomes a major problem with relationships.

I never accepted criticism well. Whenever someone disagreed with me, I'd get defensive. I felt like I was being ridiculed. I still am dealing with childhood wounds and insecurity. Although my wife loved me very much, I did not love myself. By failing to accept my own weaknesses, I could not allow myself to be loved by anyone. I felt undeserving of that love. The imaginary guy with the bat on my shoulder would push away anyone attempting to show me love. My role as a victim set me up for isolation. I dreaded a close relationship with others, including my wife, because I was afraid of being exposed as defective.

To relinquish the power these internal wounds had over me, I began a treatment plan to heal my wounds and mend my broken relationships. I had to find a way to feel safe when I was around other people. Intimacy was not possible until I understood the root of my feelings of defectiveness and inadequacy and stopped listening to the destructive voice inside my head.

Dr. Twerski explains how children feel dependent on their parents for survival and their adjustment to reality. According to Dr. Twerski, "Children must feel that their parents know what they are doing. To think that one's parents are incompetent or wrong would cause a child intolerable anxiety. If a parent abuses a child, it is easier for that child to feel he deserves the abuse than to think the parent is crazy. If a parent punishes a child for something he did not do, the child will feel, I didn't do anything wrong, but if I am punished I must somehow be bad. If a parent says something like, 'You are stupid,' the child must accept this as true. By the time the child is old enough to think for himself, his mind has already been primed and the impressions that he developed cannot be undone or disproved by logical reasoning."

One of the best ways to evaluate your childhood is to explore the feelings you had when you made a mistake. Were you allowed to blunder and learn from your mistakes or were mistakes unacceptable? When you made an error, were you able to see it as such, or did you identify yourself as defective? Since the consequence of making a mistake is unbearable pain, many of us have the need to prove we are right at all costs. If we make a mistake, we inflict inner punishment and self-hate. We then learn to conceal our feelings of defectiveness by playing roles that allow us to mask our shame, thereby losing a part of our humanity.

One of my children had a bed-wetting problem that caused him shame every time he had an accident. Once when dining out with my family years ago, I had an experience that most men can relate to. After a trip to the men's room, I zipped up my fly but not before a few drops dripped onto my pants. When I returned to the table, I quietly pointed out the spot to my son and said, "See, even Dad has accidents." He thought this was great. He believed I urinated in my pants. You could read his mind and see the way this made him feel more human for his mistakes. The downside was that he proceeded to tell the world about my experience! I did not count on this, but I did give him the message that it's OK to make mistakes. Unfortunately this was not the case with Morris.

Morris

Morris is a computer consultant in his forties, married with two children. He grew up in a household where he felt terrified about admitting to mistakes. As a result, Morris developed a distorted sense of reality that caused him and his family great heartache.

According to Morris, "The message I got as a child was that I was safe if I made myself invisible. If I rocked the boat, there was a good chance I would be physically abused by my father. My father had a terrible temper, and if I made some mistake I was terrified that he would hurt me. This created an atmosphere that told me to never admit my mistakes because the outcome had terrible consequences. On one occasion my father was driving over the Brooklyn Bridge and another driver cut him off. He gave my father the finger. My father got him to pull over, and when my father shouted at him the man rolled up his window. In a burst of anger my father actually broke the window, and the man drove away in fear for his life. I believe there also were times I feared for my own life when I felt his anger. If I made a mistake, I had the choice of admitting what I did wrong or lying. I chose to lie. My mother was supportive in many ways, but when it came to my father, she sided with him. She, too, was afraid to challenge his authority.

"My inner voice always told me I wasn't good enough, and being invisible reinforced this belief. This created the need to feel validated by others. It was as if I had a hole in my stomach and was trying to have others fill it up. It just didn't work. The same happened when my wife questioned my ability as a husband or father. I immediately flew into a rage because she touched on my defectiveness. I dreaded that my wife might leave me. To cope, I disguised myself with ego and false pride. Underneath this huge ego was a terrified little boy who protected himself by raging and bullying. Eventually my wife kicked me out of the house and told me not to return until I grew up."

Although Morris makes a good living as a computer consultant, he continues to feel inferior. Morris grew up in a family that did not tolerate mistakes. As a result, he learned it was better to lie than to admit he slipped up. Morris has begun to recognize how he projects that same intolerance onto his wife and kids. While he did not physically abuse his wife and kids, he created a family environment similar to his original family where little, if any, tolerance for mistakes is acceptable. Morris's wife threw Morris out of his house for one year. During this time, he worked on his written inventories. This situation allowed him to see how he was pushing his loved ones away.

Morris realizes how his intolerance and his obsession for being right is what pushes others away. Morris still suffers the pain of his childhood wounds, but his new willingness to surrender his impulsive anger has helped him get closer to others. The anger that once comforted him can be found in his written inventories. Over time, Morris has realized that mistakes are part of being human. As he finds compassion for himself, he finds it for others as well.

The Mask We Wear

The different masks that we hide behind are as varied as the people who wear them. They depend on our unique childhood experiences. Some people who want others to see that they have everything together wear the mask of responsibility. On the outside, these individuals appear to be highly functional and successful. On the inside, they are engaged in self-destructive behaviors designed to ease their inner turmoil.

Hank

Hank is a successful businessman with three children. According to Hank, "Some of the messages that I received from my parents during childhood were, 'You're not safe, you don't matter, you're a burden, don't tell anyone what goes on in our house.' By the time I was four years old, I had spent half my life in foster homes. I went into my first foster home when I was two years old after my mother's nervous breakdown. My father could not take care of me and my older brother because he worked full time, so the state put both of us into the foster care system. The only thing I remember about foster care was getting beaten for wetting the bed and having my face rubbed into the wet mattress like a dog. When I returned home, I had no idea when or if I would be sent to another foster home, which would be determined by my mother's mental stability. I did not feel safe in foster care, nor did I feel safe at home, because I didn't know how long I would be there. I just wanted to be left alone.

"My parents argued a lot. Once, my father hit my mother and she called the police. It was absolute chaos. My parents decided they were going to get a divorce. My father told me that if I told the truth in court about him hitting my mother, I wouldn't get to see him anymore. Tell the truth and don't get to see my father again, or lie and get to see him. What a choice! I decided to lie, but never had to go to court. My parents did not divorce, as I was told, 'for the sake of the children.' What a bunch of crap. My parents didn't do us any favors by staying married. My father slept downstairs on a foldaway couch, and my mother slept upstairs in the master bedroom. My brother and I were threatened never to tell anyone that my parents didn't sleep together. Again, my father was reinforcing the message that the truth was bad and that I should lie. I was just five years old and had spent two of those years in abusive foster homes. I would carry his message with me into all aspects of my life through adulthood. I felt shame for wanting to tell the truth, and I felt shame for lying. My life was all about shame."

Hank continues, "I continued to believe, I'd be safe if I was alone. The truth was shameful. More specifically, my true self was shameful. I always found ways to perceive myself as different. But I was different in a shaming way, always feeling 'less than' and 'not good enough.' These feelings were repeated when I continued to wet the bed until eleven years old. I lied about wetting the bed. On reflection, I'm certain that some people must have known. I always had brown teeth from taking tetracycline as an infant. Brown teeth, bed wetting, mentally unstable mother—I held onto anything to make me feel less than. I didn't know another way. I couldn't and didn't trust anybody. I only could rely on myself. I would tell myself that childhood would be the worst part of my life. When I don't need anybody I would be fine and safe. I wasn't a loner, but I didn't fit in. I always felt different. I would create excuses not to go birthday parties. I feared trusting anybody and the truth. I missed 210 days of high school. I stayed home and watched television. I pretended to be sick a lot. I just felt safer being alone."

Hank's loneliness led to many compulsive and isolating activities later in his life. He says, "I became a compulsive gambler. I was a workaholic. I was a food addict. I became addicted to pornography and masturbation. I didn't need drugs or alcohol. I could create a soothing medication for my fears with my own thoughts and actions. When I did drink alcohol, I would drink excessively to get drunk. These behaviors reinforced my shame. I believed that nobody else did these things. I had such low self-esteem on the inside, but I was so egotistical on the outside. I was driven by fears and engaged in such isolating, addictive behavior. I lived in my own world to escape and survive my childhood traumas and to keep myself or anyone from knowing the real me."

Hank put himself through college, stopped gambling with the help of Gamblers Anonymous, and became a certified accountant. He says, "I met my wife, got married, and had children. On the outside, everything looked great. On the inside, there was emptiness. I didn't think that I was worthy of having a wife. I didn't think that I was worthy of being a CPA. Eventually, I got my MBA and became the CFO of a company. I was still consumed with shame and fear. I felt like a fraud. My obsession for pornography grew. I was on the Internet for hours at a time. My wife knew nothing of this, but she did know that we weren't having sex that often. Most nights I fell asleep watching television downstairs and came to bed much later, while she fell asleep alone upstairs. I felt like a fraud. Nobody knew the real me. My childhood was something I never wanted to relive. Yet I was still driven by my fears and shame from childhood.

"Eventually, my wife saw that I had been on the Internet, looking at other women. She was devastated. I had hurt the only person who accepted me for me. I was sad and angry at myself. I feared she would divorce me. If I ever wanted true intimacy, I needed to be truthful and vulnerable and had to trust the process. This went against everything I had learned about coping with life. I did not want to be truthful and reveal who I am, nor did I want to trust another person. But, my wife was too important, so I tried to be open and honest. The fear of losing her was more powerful than the fear of letting her see the true me. I didn't want to trust my sponsor, but I needed to trust him and did so because he had walked in my shoes. He seemed happy and serene. I needed that. "

Hank's inner voice told him to avoid intimacy and being vulnerable in front of others. Hank erected huge barriers to keep others away. Although kind and generous, he was consumed with shame, inadequacy, and his overarching fear of being vulnerable, which prevented him from letting down his guard. He was a prisoner to all of the messages inside his head, which included, *people weren't safe, he didn't matter to anyone, he was a burden, and never tell anyone how you feel.* Not until faced with the devastation that occurred after his wife learned of his secret addiction to Internet pornography was he able to admit his problem and begin the journey to freedom.

Hank continually wrestled to keep his secret fears from surfacing. As he opened up to his support group, he began to feel more comfortable with himself and others. He came to realize that he did not have to be perfect to be accepted. The more he was willing to accept himself, the more he was able to see the corrupt nature of his old beliefs. He began to recognize and surrender his fears. As this happened, he began to rely less on the mask he used to wear to protect himself.

Mask of Victimhood

There are people who wear the mask of victimhood. They have a hard time functioning and their problems are more obvious to the world. Jobs are lost, home utilities are turned off, and marriages are ruined. Yet, it is always someone else's fault.

Murray

Murray is in his forties, married, and has one child. According to Murray, "My parents worked all day, so when school was over, I went straight to my grandparents' home. When I eventually got home, it was late at night and time to go to sleep. When I saw my parents, they spent most of their time yelling at each other. I remember feeling I had to live up to my father's expectations or risk making him unhappy. As a child, I attended a musical school for gifted children. I had to prepare a program that was graded twice a year. It was very important for me to get excellent grades. When I received anything less, I felt like a failure.

"I loved being with my grandparents. I used to read with my grandfather and felt that he paid attention to me. When my grandparents passed away I was devastated. But, when my mother died, I really didn't feel a great loss. I started hitchhiking because I wanted to travel to new places. One day I returned home and thought I would surprise my father. As he opened the door to let me in, he appeared disappointed. He said he answered the door because he thought it was my sister. He then turned and walked away. To help cope with the feelings of rejection, I started to drink and take drugs. I always hated alcohol, but used it to medicate the pain I was feeling inside."

Murray says he realized that whenever anyone ignored him, he would initially shut down inside, but later rage out at whoever touched this wound. He says, "When my boss or wife ignored me, I felt like a victim. I realized I was angry, but I didn't realize where this anger came from. I blamed them. In the past, I held a job for many years without getting a raise. I was always making excuses for why I stayed with this job. Every time I thought about leaving, my fear would tell me that things would get better. My bosses took advantage of me. I felt like a victim, but instead of taking responsibility for my actions, I just got angry with them. I would vent my anger with my sponsor. When he suggested I find another job, I didn't want to consider it. I also wanted to start my own photography business, but was so paralyzed by fear I couldn't move. My support group kept pushing me to do a few jobs for free as a way of getting my work out to the public. I had enough trust in them to do as I was told."

When Murray started to look for a job, his inner voice of fear spoke. He told himself that he would never find a better job. He had visions of eventually becoming unemployed and his family starving to death. Though he hated his present job, he was afraid of looking elsewhere. His inner voice kept telling him the old job was not so bad, but the facts proved otherwise. Murray pointed the finger at everyone but himself. He promised to keep going on interviews whether he wanted to or not. Through persistence, eventually he did find a better job.

His need to be right was destroying him. The more willing Murray was to complete the written inventories of Twelve Step work, the more he became aware of the disruption in his life caused by his negative inner voice. He realized how much of his fear was manufactured by his warden, who never really wanted him to find happiness in a better job. His courage to take direction would eventually allow him to say no to the imaginary fears the warden created.

Mask of Superiority

Some people wear the mask of superiority. These know-it-alls have little empathy for others and harshly judge others. This disguises the self-recrimination these people feel inside. The following story about Paul shows how he underwent the greatest devastation a father could have and how it ultimately removed his mask of superiority. After life threw a devastating curve, he finally asked for help.

Paul

Paul is a successful businessman in his early fifties. He has been married twice with a child from his first marriage and two from his second. According to Paul, "I grew up in a very religious family with a lot of discipline. I guess my family loved me but I felt very controlled by them. I was always defiant of authority. If they wanted me to do A, I would do B. This defiant voice permeated every one of my relationships. Even as a child, I never wanted to conform to anything. I could have gotten A's in school, but I had to do things my way. I married very young and had one daughter. The marriage did not last long. I remarried and had two more children. Most of my life was plagued by one addiction after another. I would go to Twelve Step programs, but they never helped. I had to do things my way.

"Eventually, my drug of choice turned to prostitutes. One night I was cruising for a prostitute and saw my daughter, age twenty, on the streets. I knew she had problems with drugs, but I never thought it would bring her to prostitution. I was devastated. I took her to an inpatient rehabilitation center for help. She tested positive for HIV. This was at a time when HIV was a death sentence. A second and third test came back negative. I learned that I couldn't give her what I didn't have myself. Every time I got the urge to become defiant, I instead chose to obey. Listening to others for guidance and support lifted a tremendous weight from my shoulders. I surrendered. It's a wonderful feeling to know there are people in this world who are there for me, no matter what. I thank God for my support system because I don't know what I would have done without them."

The devastating reality of seeing his daughter on the streets paved the way for a miracle. This miracle caused a transformation in Paul that enabled him to willingly give up control. His willingness to listen to others instead of resisting them has allowed him to enjoy a newfound serenity. Life has not been easy for Paul, but he is happier today than he has been in all the years I have known him. While he attempts to give his daughter all the love and acceptance that he was never able to give her as a child, he understands that some things are beyond his control. He still prays and asks God to watch over her. He knows now that he does not have to face his pain alone.

Mask of Uniqueness

The mask of uniqueness proclaims to the world, "I am unique; no one is like me, nor can anyone possibly understand me." People wear this mask as a way of keeping others at a distance. Consequently, they remain isolated from other people. The warden's message is very clear: *Do not trust anyone, ever.*

Jimmy

Jimmy is a single man in his forties. According to Jimmy, "I grew up in a poor household and felt ashamed as a child. I believed that people saw my family as trash because of our poverty and our filth. I received mixed signals from my father. He was warm at times, but when drunk, he was verbally abusive. I would confide in him about things that were going on in my life, but as soon as he drank, he would use anything I told him against me. My mother was very needy and I felt that it was my responsibility to take care of her. She seldom interacted with my father, so in many ways I was closer to her then he was. The message was clear, my needs could only be met if I took care of her needs first.

"As I grew older, I started to realize I was attracted to men. This created tremendous self-hatred. I loathed myself for being a homosexual and despised God for allowing this to happen. Eventually, life became so unbearable I contemplated suicide. When I finally asked for help, I was lucky to find someone who guided me toward self-acceptance. I did written inventories on my childhood wounds. I discovered that I not only hated men who were proud to be gay, but I also hated gay men who were angry for being gay. I also hated heterosexual men because they weren't gay. I set myself up to dislike everyone, because I really hated myself. I believed the world saw me in the same negative way. My feeling of uniqueness toward the world ensured me that I could remain a victim. My uniqueness also created a fear of people. Even as I started to join groups and fellowships, I would always find a way to make myself feel different from everyone else."

Jimmy found it hard to believe that others would accept him. He says, "I tried my best to convince people that I wasn't worthy of their friendship. When I isolated myself from everyone in the support network, I still got phone calls telling me I was loved and missed. These people saw through my mask and realized the pain I was in. Eventually, I would ask, 'Why are you always there for me?' The answer was always the same, 'Because I don't see you the way you see yourself.'

"I made up stories about the ways I was different or unique from others. Through the help of my support group, I began to feel connected to the human race. Although this feeling of connection was short lived, I was told to be patient with my progress. As time has passed, I have become more aware of the ways my destructive thinking has pulled me away from all types of people. I see that whenever I was in a social setting, I always focused on the person or situation that made me feel unique and different. I would concentrate on the way people have disappointed me. Self-acceptance has come slowly for me, but I have increased my trust in others. Although I hate to admit this to others, the more I allow people to accept me, the easier it is to accept myself. I keep moving forward while pursuing the necessary steps in finding self-acceptance, especially when my fear of people pulls me back."

Jimmy still fights the voices of self-loathing, but he demonstrates courage by fighting his biggest demon, the fear of other people. When he is making up a negative story in his head about someone, he calls that person to find out if the story is true or distorted. That takes courage to make those phone calls. The more he attempts to connect with others, the more he sees that people are not there to hurt him. The reality is, they do not see him the way he feels inside. He can only conclude this by finding courage to confront his demons and challenge his fears.

These stories show the different ways that people choose to wear masks. Some people may wear one or more masks, depending on the roles they think they need to play in front of certain people. Still, beneath the surface of these masks lie the same wounds of inferiority and defectiveness. The masks help shield them from a world in which they feel inadequate and unable to participate.

No matter what mask we wear, the feelings of defectiveness and inferiority are similar. People who wear a mask of responsibility may have a tougher time asking for help, because they are convinced that they are solely accountable for their success.

I can relate to the person who wears the mask of responsibility. For me, success in business gave me false confidence. I thought I needed no one to succeed, not even God. Individual achievement may work when it comes to obtaining material things, but it will not help to fill that empty void that resides deep within you.

Emotional Wounds Beneath the Masks

Childhood wounds are acerbated especially when dealing with any form of rejection, abandonment, or criticism. Those wounds are rooted in the violation of basic trust that we had placed in our parents and other loved ones. To protect myself from pain, my inner voice supplied me with a barrier to keep others outside while limiting my chances of being exposed to potential harm and criticism. Intimacy, vulnerability, trust, and pain were to be avoided at all cost.

In group therapy, I met a man who had an abusive, alcoholic father. As a child, he would confide in his father when he was sober. He shared both weaknesses and disappointments with him. In the beginning, the sober dad would listen to his son's story and would be occasionally supportive. However, during an alcoholic rage his father would turn against him. He would yell and put down his son for being weak. The message he sent to his son was loud and clear: Do not be emotionally vulnerable with other men by sharing your weaknesses; they will only betray and hurt you badly by using your weaknesses against you." I encouraged him to speak up at group and share his story, but he was terrified to do so. He would never speak up or share, and frequently dashed out of the group as soon as it ended.

Another man in group struck back verbally to keep people from getting too close. Knowing his short fuse for anger, nobody dared to challenge or confront him. The reopening of old internal wounds was so painful that he would go to any length to protect these wounds from exposure.

Healthy Treatment for Wounds

I never believed that others would accept me for who I was, yet over time I learned to let go of those fears as I developed closer relationships to people. By finding a group willing to accept me with all my shortcomings, I grew in self-acceptance and found the courage to say no to the voice inside my head. I learned to expose my wounds and to feel part of a fellowship for the first time in my life. *Self-disclosure which leads to intimacy and greater self-acceptance is vital to healing.* That is why releasing secrets, shame, and guilt is so important. The wounds can be treated by acknowledging your past, how you were hurt, and how you may have hurt others. Only then can the process of healing begin. I began by first sharing my wounds with others. As I grew in humility, I grew in self-acceptance. If I can accept myself then I am capable of accepting others. I humbly ask, "How can I support or help you?" Rather than fix other people's problems, I let them know I'm there for them, no matter what.

Before my recovery and healing began, I had far less empathy for others. When my emotional wounds were triggered, it was hard for me to feel the pain of others. However, as I begin to heal, I noticed how much easier it was to identify with the pain of others. This is why it is so vital to first address your own internal wounds before helping others. Until then, it will be difficult to think beyond yourself.

Gratitude is another indicator of healing. I always wanted to be grateful for the things I had, but gratitude never came easy. I was always amazed how some people with so little could be grateful, while others with so much took everything for granted. As I began to heal, I realized how little material things really mattered. Pain is an internal problem and cannot be eased by external objects. Gratitude does not happen overnight. It takes time. I was so impatient with the entire healing process. I expected instant gratification, but it doesn't work that way. I needed to follow the recommendations of others. As I heeded their advice, my feeling of gratitude came naturally. I felt thankful for what I had, and less resentful and victimized for what I did not have. My support group gave me strength.

Not Giving Away My Power to Others

In the past it was easy to predict that if anyone pushed my buttons, I would lash out in anger. But, as I began to heal I no longer permitted anyone that power over me. Anger is a natural emotion, but now I have healthier ways to cope. I reach out to others and ask for help or guidance when I need it. I am no longer the victim. I no longer try to control my wife. Now I am comfortable surrendering control and thinking only about being present in the moment so I can more fully empathize with my wife's feelings and needs.

The most challenging test for me is when my wife brings up my past compulsions. I would rather focus on her shortcomings than mine. But, there is no denying that I hurt her profoundly, and that I need to confront the issues with her without lapsing into self-pity or self-victimization. To be a better husband and father, I had to get past the notion of being like a defective person. I had to avoid listening to the little voice inside my head and learn to accept myself, both the good and the bad, and to understand that I am not perfect. People with deep childhood wounds tend to be selfish in nature, not because they are bad but because selfishness develops as a survival instinct. When I accept my imperfections instead of berating myself, I find the willingness to work on my character defects. In addition, with acceptance comes the ability to find empathy and compassion for my wife and others. Although I never will know the full extent of the pain I caused her, I can show her my sincere regret. We cannot undo the past. But, we have the power to transform our future by learning from past mistakes. Today, we still have our disagreements, but we've learned how to declare a truce and bring our issues to our individual support groups. We no longer focus on trying to fix each other. In looking at our own character defects and wounds, we pray for strength and for each of us to find our individual paths.

Chapter Six: Silencing the Negative Inner Voices

The inner voices, created from the childhood emotional wounds,
can distract us from the work of healing.

80C3

My own childhood wounds created such an inner void that
I tried to fill the emptiness with one harmful solution after another.
When the consequences of one became too much, I would replace it
with another. I believe that my destructive behaviors were never the
real problem. My problem was my victim thinking, led by the little
voice inside my head. Both guided me toward harmful behaviors.
These negative messages not only distorted my perception of reality,
but also my ability to do the right thing. This warped sense of reality
led me to engage in destructive behaviors, often hurting the people I
loved most in order to ease the internal pain. I was living in a state of
victimhood and had developed an attitude of "me versus the world."

For this reason, I needed to find people who I could trust to
be there for me. These people could point out my victim thinking and
that destructive inner voice. Without them, my false beliefs about life
and myself would lead me toward isolation. That inner voice would
try to control my thinking, and my thinking, in turn, would control
my actions. Consequently, my shame would become so great that I
would never allow anyone to get close to me. The guy on my shoulder
would be swinging away constantly, reminding me of my faults and
causing me to spiral out of control into even greater self-loathing and
shame. My victim thinking convinced me that in order to feel good
about myself, I always had to be right.

A Good Person Doesn't Make Mistakes

For me, mistakes were inexcusable and had to be hidden at
all costs. I couldn't imagine exposing my shortcomings because that

would only reinforce my feelings of inadequacy. A healthy, compassionate voice would have told me that mistakes were a part of life. But that voice did not exist for me. I felt that I needed to hide my failings, which made it difficult to listen to anyone, especially when I was criticized. My inability to listen also contributed to my victim mentality. Eventually, I came to understand that I needed to find the courage to admit my wrongdoings and ask for help. The asking-for-help option was tough for me. My victim thinking, so deeply embedded, was more difficult to surrender than even my destructive behaviors. While my destructive behaviors took a huge toll on my life, my victim thinking fueled the flames of self-righteousness. Victim thinking was the root of the problem, even though the destructive behaviors needed to be isolated before I could begin treatment.

A Good Person Does Not Get Angry with His Parents

Dr. Twerski talks about a psychological maneuver known as *displacement*. According to Dr. Twerski, "The subconscious mind diverts or redirects ideas and feelings. It is as if a guided missile went off course, aiming for the wrong target. People at the control center can change its course, so it lands in an uninhabited area where it can do no harm."

Dr. Twerski further explains, "Suppose that a child develops angry feelings toward a parent. The guilt from such feelings may be very intense. To protect the child from the distress of feeling guilty, the subconscious mind represses this anger. That is, it takes it out of the person's conscious mind so he no longer is aware of his anger. But the subconscious mind cannot eradicate this angry feeling and stores it away, deep in the subbasement where it can hibernate for years."

The voice that tells us we have no right to get angry at our parents is responsible for a lot of inner turmoil. When we do things for our parents out of guilt or manipulation, eventually we turn the anger on ourselves and them. It's not easy to go to your parents and say, "This is your baggage, not mine." But, that may be necessary. The fear of saying no to our parents is carried into our adult life through our relationship with spouses, children, other family members, and friends.

Rory

Rory is single and in his forties. According to Rory, "I grew up in rural South Carolina, the first of three sons born to very young parents. My father worked double shifts leaving my mother and me alone at night. To protect our family and ease my mother's mind, my father kept a pistol in the attic that could be fired by pulling a string to scare away intruders. I remember long nights being as scared as my mother. The difference was, when my father got home she was relieved, but I was not. I was close to my mother then, but the man who was my father I saw mostly on Sundays. He seemed as frightening to me as the burglars and psychos in my mother's mind.

"Both my parents were strict disciplinarians with little tolerance for disobedience or sassing. My father's reaction was usually swift and direct. A flash of anger led to a painful and humiliating spanking. My mother used manipulation to discipline me. In addition to warning me of my father's reaction when he got home, she'd often use guilt to manipulate me. She would say, 'After all your daddy and I do for you, this is how you act?'"

Rory says he was a mama's boy from the start and wanted to please her. He continues, "But early on, I also began to distrust her. When I was very young I told my mother that I wished my father would die so I could marry her. The next day she told me never to say that again. She said that when she told my father he replied, 'If he ever says that again I will castrate him.'

"I learned two things from this experience. First, my father was dangerous and my mother could not be trusted. Therefore, I needed to keep my thoughts and feelings to myself. No matter what I felt, it was easiest to say, 'Yes, I'll do it,' even if I had no idea how I could and had no intention to follow through. At times, my mother would forget what she'd told me to do, and occasionally my father would be in a lighthearted mood and let it go. I found that saying 'Yes' had its rewards. Being the good little boy brought my mother great pride. I savored the pats on the back from grandparents and other relatives when I excelled at school or was in a church performance."

Rory says his only real escape in childhood was his imagination. "I became a chronic daydreamer. In my dreams I could be myself and do as I pleased, unlike in the real world. Gradually the imaginary world became preferable to reality. When the real world became too much, I took refuge in my fantasies. My escape into the fantasy world increased as the fantasies became sexual.

"In day-to-day life, I became a natural born follower. I felt like a stow-away on a passenger train speeding off to some unknown destination. Everyone but me seemed to know where they were going and acted as if it was their right to be there. My goal was to fake it, to play along, hoping that I wouldn't be thrown off at the next station. This is how I went through life, until I sought help.

"As I let others in I have experienced many changes and received many gifts. For the first time in my life, I feel at ease in social situations. I recognize many of the distorted thoughts and beliefs I have for what they are. I still believe that if I say 'No' to someone that I'll disappoint them and they'll end up rejecting me, making my life unbearable. The feeling is so strong that I often have trouble identifying what it is that I want or need. With the help of others I am learning to challenge this fear. I'm learning that it's OK to say 'No' and often better than the pain of selling myself out and hating myself for doing it."

Rory has been a caretaker his whole life. He is afraid to say no and is worried about being criticized if he does so. His inner voice tells him a good son never disappoints his parents by saying no. It was a setup for resentment since caretakers often assume more than they can handle and become overwhelmed. Sometimes they may even feel they deserve payback for their efforts, which furthers resentment. I shared my own struggles with Rory about my difficulty of saying no to others. I now would rather someone dislike me for telling the truth, than for believing I'm someone I'm not. Saying no may be hard at first, but in time it gets easier. Our inner voice has the power to dominate our thinking and keep us from reaching our true potential. It tells us that people would never accept us as we truly are. We begin to believe that the world owes us big time, which can lead to destructive entitlement, hopelessness, and despair.

Inner Voices of Failure

Many of us are completely overwhelmed because our inner voice tells us we are failures. I worked with a woman who felt ashamed because of her messy house. It symbolized how she felt about herself. By keeping it messy, she continued to isolate and keep people away. Each time she envisioned the overwhelming task of cleaning she began to feel worthless. She said she could commit to doing housework for one hour a day. I suggested she break the job down into manageable tasks, doing one small portion at a time over that hour. I would call her at the beginning of the hour and at the end of the hour to make sure she kept her commitment. It worked. Having a support group persuaded her to take the necessary action.

I Don't Deserve Happiness

Dr. Twerski says the most damaging misconception is the development of unwarranted feelings of self-negativity. According to Dr. Twerski, "The person who, in reality, is quite capable but thinks of herself as inferior in one or more ways will have a difficult time adjusting in life. A person can adjust optimally to reality only with a valid perception of realism, whereas a deluded person will not adjust. If a destitute person fancies herself wealthy and makes unrealistic purchases, she is certain to get into trouble. If a person is bright, handsome, and personable but thinks of himself as dull, unattractive, and unlikable, this person is destined to a lifetime of problems unless he can recognize his dilemma and get the proper help."

Dr. Twerski explains that we generally assume that other people see things just as we see them. He says, "If we see a garbage dump, we will assume that everyone looking at it will also see a garbage dump and not a bed of beautiful roses. Similarly, if we perceive ourselves as negative, we will assume it is how others see us and we will relate to them accordingly."

Children who receive negative messages grow up sabotaging happiness. They are attracted to people who will treat them poorly and push away people who treat them kindly. Many religious people struggle the most before their holy days. In times of worship, we may find ourselves alone with our own thoughts, when the reality of our consequences becomes clearer. During my destructive years, my self-hate increased on Sundays and holidays, because I didn't go to work. Sunday was the day I had nothing to do but think of who I was. During holidays, all I could feel was emptiness inside. I would shut down emotionally and could not understand how I could feel so alone in the company of the people I loved most. My wife would notice my sadness. She tried to gently cheer me up, but nothing she did would ease my pain. In time, as I continued to work my recovery program, my gratitude increased and I felt more deserving of happiness.

Feelings of hopelessness can pass from generation to generation. Many times these inner voices are so subtle that the person is unaware that he or she is setting himself up for pain. One such person is Mario. Mario rarely felt that deep sense of security that most children take for granted. He grew up in a dysfunctional home where chaos was the norm. The battle zone made it easy for him to avoid his feelings. He felt that he did not deserve to be happy, so he played out that role by sabotaging everything good that came his way.

Mario

Mario is married with two children. According to Mario, "Everyone in my family led a secret life. My parents divorced because of my father's infidelity. My mother was unfaithful to her new husband after she remarried. Whenever I told my sister something in confidence, she betrayed me. Believing that nobody would be there for me, I felt frightened and alone. I tried to live up to my stepfather's expectations by playing sports even though I wasn't interested. A voice told me that I had to be who he wanted me to be. As I grew older, I could never stick to anything for too long, especially if things started to get tough. I had become a very angry person. While I never physically hurt anyone, I was prone to overreact. For example, I would get very angry at my wife when the house was messy. I would become paranoid when she would go out with her sister, believing that she was having an affair with another man. Then I'd have to apologize for not trusting her.

"I did this with my boss too. I was a good money earner, but when he gave jobs to other employees, I thought he was telling me I was no good. All of these things brought out a very deep feeling of dread. I felt so let down and angry that I started gambling to ease the pain."

When Mario could no longer live with the anger and the constant need to apologize, he decided to get help by joining a support group and asking the group leader for help. He says, "I felt ashamed even asking for help. My stepfather's voice was in my head telling me I would be judged if I shared my weaknesses with other people. I learned a lot about myself. When my wife didn't listen to me or my boss overlooked me, I realized how humiliated I felt and wanted them to feel the same way. I needed more than awareness, however. I needed to start making changes in order to deal with my anger and resentment. My sponsor was my savior. I was told to call him as soon as I got angry and take my anger out on him instead of others. He also wanted to hear all of my thoughts, no matter how horrible they were. Today, I can't say my anger is completely gone, but as I stay away from my addictions and keep talking about my difficulties, I definitely have found more peace in my life."

As comfortable as Mario was with me, he still believed I saw him as he viewed himself. His warden led him to this destructive way of thinking, making him believe he needed to act the way others expected or they wouldn't accept him. Over time and with help, Mario was able to guard against such harmful thinking. He learned that the stories he was making up about others were untrue. When he was convinced of this, good things started to happen. He started up his own company and called me for guidance whenever he felt discouraged. Even though his business was doing well, the good times were not enough to keep him from going astray. In his business, he needed to make forty calls a day, but at times he had no strength for even one. I asked him how many calls he could make in an hour, and he said eight to ten. I suggested he make the calls and get back to me one hour later. We did this on an hourly basis until he ultimately attained his goal. With each passing hour, his attitude improved. Today, he continues to call me when he uncovers something too troubling to process alone. He takes comfort from his newly adopted voices that tell him he no longer needs to face his difficulties alone.

Like Mario, I also had to examine how my childhood messages affect the role I play as an adult. I now know that I can choose to listen and share my own experience, but I do not need to attempt to resolve the problems of others. Learning how to let go of the expectations of others takes time, patience, and practice. Accepting people for where they are in life rather than where I *think* they should be can be difficult. I still slip up and get angry at times when people aren't acting and thinking the way I feel they should. When this happens, I pause and try to examine what my role was in the incident, rather than focusing blame on the other person who I thought triggered my anger.

Destructive Voices

Dr. Twerski explains the ways that intrusive messages of childhood can direct our thinking as adults. According to Dr. Twerski, "When confronted with challenge, there are only two possible ways to react: we can either cope or escape. The decision is made based on how we view the challenge. If we think we're capable of coping then we're likely to try. But if we view the challenge as overwhelming, then we probably will choose to escape. It follows that if a person has unwarranted feelings of inferiority and inadequacy, he or she will seek escape even if that challenge may be within his or her ability to cope."

According to Dr. Twerski, "Addictions of all types are escapes from what we perceive to be unmanageable realities. In reality, addictive behavior is too often the result of our misguided thinking that we are inadequate or unworthy and must therefore take the easy way out."

Jerry's story demonstrates how difficult it is to trust. When I first met him, he was so fearful of trusting me that he wouldn't tell me his real name for several months.

Jerry

Jerry is a thirty-year-old married man who grew up in a religious household. According to Jerry, "I was always expected to be a good boy, which in my family translated into doing everything perfect. The opposite also held true. If I wasn't perfect, then I was bad. When

I graduated from elementary school my father said to my mother in front of me, "Why can't my son get honors like everyone else?" I was taught that people have to recognize you and respect you, and if they don't then you're worthless. Based upon on this faulty value system, I attempted to build my own self-worth by chasing down compliments and lying about my accomplishments.

"In my mind it was better to project a false image than to be honest about how I felt. I believed that if I'm not going to succeed then there is no sense in trying, because it's what you achieve that's important, not who you are. And since you're going to fail anyway, why bother trying? I used to study and learn the Holy Torah and felt somewhat accomplished. As time went on, negative voices convinced me that I was hopeless and I gave it up. I felt so unworthy and afraid that I couldn't accomplish that perfect status or image, so why even try?"

Jerry says he had a poor self-image and did not feel accepted by others. He says, "It seemed like others were always judging me, and I wasn't sure if this was a distortion or reality. I finally became so sick of myself that I joined a support group. Because I didn't trust anyone, I gave them a false name. Eventually, I began to reveal more of myself to the group. They never judged me or made me feel I wasn't good enough for them. They allowed me to share my difficulties at work and even helped me look for a new job. I was ashamed to disclose my real name to them until months later. I was very surprised to find out that they forgave me and accepted my action because they understood my fear in trusting others. They also helped me deal with the relationship with my wife. Whenever I was afraid to talk to her about my painful feelings, they reminded me that my wife would never judge me the way my parents did when I was a child. In time, I learned to put my trust in others."

As I spoke to Jerry about my own difficulties, including my struggle with trust, he became more comfortable with me. Jerry eventually became more willing to open up to our group. Unlike his family, the support group provides a safe haven for him to share his feelings. The more trusting he becomes, the more he can recognize that he is no different than anyone else.

Before we can heal, we need to process our personal struggle. At the heart of the struggle is the person who must place his or her faith and trust in the support group. The voice of destructive entitlement wants us to see our behavior as the primary solution to our problems. Our inner voice may drown out all reasonable thoughts, causing us to be like spoiled children who constantly demand attention and instant gratification.

There are certain themes that can be found in the destructive inner voice that drives our pain. These unhealthy message are

- You do not need others.
- You can behave as you please.
- Nobody will ever be there for you.
- You are different from others.
- You are a victim.
- Your false pride is acceptable.

You Do Not Need Others

The little voice inside our head becomes very angry when we refuse to listen. In turn, our healthy relationships are sabotaged. The closer we get to those who can help us, the more this voice tries to push them away. There are kind and loving people who would gladly help us if we asked for it. The fear of asking for help can be terrifying for some of us. If we ask for help and are rejected, we are bombarded with shame and unworthiness. We need these compassionate, supportive voices to overcome the voice that guides us toward harmful behaviors.

You Can Behave as You Please

The voice of destructive entitlement tells us we have the right to act the way we want to, but fails to inform us of the resulting consequences. This is distorted thinking at its best. Whenever I slip back into old habits, the only thing that remains is shame and self-hatred. My inner voice preys on my fears and insecurities and reinforces the belief that something is wrong with me, that I am undeserving of love, and will eventually end up alone and hopeless.

Mel's story illustrates what can happen when these voices are out of control.

Mel

Mel is single and in his late twenties. According to Mel, "When I was three years old my mother died. I believed she died because I wasn't important to her. As an adolescent, I knew how silly this was but I still felt abandoned. My father had a volatile temper and was having a difficult time coping without my mother. He would take out his anger on me. He would yell at me when I didn't take out the garbage or clean my room, or when I failed to wash the dishes and do the laundry. I started to believe that I couldn't do anything right or that I didn't matter. Once when a young man babysat me when I was eight and my brother was five, he started to masturbate in front of us. When my father got home my brother told him about it. My father beat this kid to a pulp. I actually thought he killed him. Whether my father was right or wrong, his display of anger scared me to death.

"As I got older, I avoided intimate relationships, because I dreaded being hurt or abandoned. Even though I hated being alone, I never allowed myself to get close to anyone. Instead, I would go to strip clubs or masturbate to pornography online. Whether things were going good or bad, I felt entitled. Shame kept me inside my head and I never let anyone into the horrible world in which I lived. The insanity of my thoughts and actions were overwhelming. I felt completely hopeless and thought about suicide."

Mel says he didn't fully understand his situation until he found a support group and began sharing his troubles with others. He says, "In group I learned about acceptance, unconditional love, and everything else that I missed in childhood. My leader explained that when I get angry with someone, it is because that person has touched some deep painful wound, which creates a voice that tells me I'm worthless. Without this guidance, I would continue to react in the same destructive manner that had isolated me from the world. I know I need help and can't do it on my own. In the beginning, phone calls with supportive group members were difficult, but I was encouraged to continue. I have also learned that isolation, manufactured fear, and false pride are liabilities, and that by sabotaging everything good in my life I was setting myself up to be a victim. I now know my fears were out of whack because of my abandonment issues, although it was me who always found a way to push others away. When things were going well with my girlfriend, I found some excuse to get angry which resulted in her distancing herself from me. My group and written inventories have allowed me to recover from my wounds and discover my true identity. I no longer feel the emptiness inside that I always lived with."

Mel feared intimacy because of his abandonment issues. He continued to search for love in places where intimacy could never be found. His fear of women was precipitated by the death of his mother at a very young age. These fears played out a story which always ended with loneliness. His fear of being alone was so profound that he created enough mental evidence that it became real to him. Besides the abandonment issues Mel had with his mother, he also had a father guided by anger and victim thinking. His parents' relationship was built on avoidance and shame. Mel never had a chance to say no to the journey he was on. He considered prostitutes and massage parlors his only true relationships. To Mel they were safe, certainly free from any emotional attachment. All this came out in his written inventories.

Today, Mel is involved in a healthy relationship in which he feels safe. He still doesn't feel that he deserves happiness. He fears that he will be abandoned, but as long as he stays connected to his support group he will be OK.

Nobody Will Ever Be There for You

The voice of entitlement is cunning. Repeatedly it declares, "Nobody will ever be there for you but me." It tells us we must listen to our inner voice if we want to be happy and ignore the needs of the people we care about most. It says, "If your spouse really loved you, he or she would show it more," or, "If your friends really cared, they would treat you better." It compels us to be overly judgmental while being a victim. This voice makes us distrustful of others so we are unable to distinguish healthy boundaries between right and wrong.

You Are Different from Others

The voice inside our head uses any difference with others to drive a wedge between us and them. These differences may be age, ethnic background, religion, or sexual orientation. No matter how we look on the outside, on the inside we share countless similarities. Moreover, we all want peace and happiness despite our addictions to alcohol, drugs, excessive working, eating, gambling, or sex. The question that must be asked is, "When I am in discomfort do I *depend* on my support group for help or do I run to my addictions instead?" If one is an addict their addictive voice will always try to take them back to their addiction as their solution.

You Are a Victim

Our inner voice informs us that the world will always disappoint us. People won't do what we expect of them. In turn, this creates self-pity and sets us up as the victim. This leads to the feeling of self-righteousness, which suggests our problems stem from the shortcomings of others. Sometimes the voice will team up with self-hate to make us feel worthless inside and once again separate us from others. Many of us are so comfortable with this message that we end up wearing the mask of victimhood for our entire lives.

Your False Pride Is Acceptable

Even though our inner voice will congratulate us on a job well done, we need to be careful. It may be an opportunity created simply to gain back control of our old behavior. As we grow, we learn that we don't need to listen to the destructive messages from the past. As we begin to embrace our support group, we begin to notice, in time, that our inner voice becomes quieter. The destructive messages from our past gradually are replaced with the new, more compassionate thoughts we have learned. I accept my destructive inner voice as being a part of who I am. Rather than empowering the voice, I now say "Thank you for sharing," then reach out to my support system for guidance.

Chapter Seven: Trusting Others

Please help me, but don't get too close.

ℰℐℂℛ

There is no program of recovery or growth that is painless. All of us will find reasons to avoid this kind of inner pain. Before I could place my trust in others, I needed to take three steps. First, I had to discover the nature of my problem. Second, I had to find a solution. Third, I had to work out a plan of action. Only by trusting other people could I successfully process new information into my belief system. In so doing, I was able to purge myself of some of those negative beliefs.

The Problem

During my years of acting-out behavior, I often repeated the words, "Please God, protect me from myself." I felt disconnected from any type of environment that promised healing or recovery. I felt superior *and* inferior. Although I knew I needed help, I dreaded the vulnerability of sharing my innermost feelings. Intimacy was too painful. The abandonment I felt in childhood left deep scars. I couldn't risk getting hurt again. This created a self-centered belief system that did not permit trust.

My inner voice told me that I could not survive without my habit, even though I understood this was insane. The addiction kept me in chains. A part of me hated myself so much I frequently thought about suicide. I couldn't look at myself in the mirror anymore. I wanted the pain of living to go away. What stopped me was thinking about my family and what the wounds of suicide would inflict on them.

Still, I needed to feel in control of my healing process. The more fearful I was, the more I felt the need to control the process. I wanted to heal, but I was neither ready nor willing to take the appropriate steps. Not only did I need the willingness to *ask for help,* but also I needed the willingness to *accept direction* when help was offered.

The Solution

My first task was to find a therapist or a support group that satisfied my needs even if I felt it was a waste of my time. When I realized that I was no different from others seeking help, I became more willing to remove my mask in order to heal. As I attended more groups, I gradually shed the outer layers of shame that had isolated me from the world.

Because of a continuing power struggle between the new voice of hope and the old voice of intrusion, I needed to attend these groups faithfully. Trusting others was difficult, but it was necessary for me to escape the pain of loneliness that I had lived with all my life. When I understood this, I stopped fighting.

Working the Solution

In high school, I had a physical education teacher who taught us the three requirements for obtaining a good grade. He was very clear: "First, do what you are told. Second, do what you are told. And third, do what you are told." To heal your wounds, you must do as you're told by your sponsor, therapist, or group. Don't listen to those destructive inner voices from the past. Healing requires the ultimate self-discipline.

My biggest obstacle was giving up control. This is the ultimate task for a control freak like me. My first assignment was to trust my therapist and support group. They decided I should disclose to my wife the details of my infidelity. This advice might not be appropriate for everyone, but it was the right advice for me. It would also become my most difficult and challenging test. I became defensive and was scared of my wife's reaction. I thought she would never forgive me. I reluctantly did what I was told while putting my faith in the power of the group and my therapist.

Disclosure

I had an appointment with my wife at her therapist's office. Her therapist was experienced with disclosure techniques. I kept telling myself that, in time, the truth would bring us closer and that she would eventually forgive me. With no more secrets we could begin a life of intimacy that up until now had been impossible because of my indiscretions. I didn't know whether my disclosure would to be more frightening for me or for her. I was terrified.

I prayed that she already knew everything that I was about to tell her. When I began to disclose, she started to scream. I was gripped with anguish but had no place to run. I could not rationalize my actions or deny the pain I caused the woman I loved. I broke down. It was the first time my wife had seen me cry. Years later, she told me that it was my tears that saved our marriage. I thank God for this special woman who was able to see my pain in the middle of her own agony. The therapist kept urging me to be as candid as possible. She told my wife that my disclosure was prompted by my love for her, which was why I wanted to turn my life around. In the upcoming sessions my wife told me, "Our marriage was a lie." Initially, I couldn't understand this. I knew I loved my family more than anything in my life. I would run in front of a bus for any of them and they knew this. However, in time, I understood exactly what she meant. If she had done to me what I had done to her, I would have felt the same way she did.

Her grief, at times, bordered on rage, and this would continue for more than a year. Telling her how profoundly sorry I was meant nothing. I had to back up my words with action. There were days she accused me of things that I did not do. There were also nights when her pain hit such a crescendo that she shut me out. Throughout this, I concluded that my place was to be there for her when she wanted to talk and to give her space when she needed to be alone. She was experiencing a roller coaster of emotions. One day her roller coaster would plummet to resentment and anger, and the next day it would lift toward forgiveness. It was a confusing and turbulent time. Her world was turned upside down and she needed someone to hold her up.

My faith that everything would work out for the best is what kept me going. During the most stressful times she pumped me with questions. On those occasions, I would call on my group for moral support and the strength to endure. Sometimes, my victim mentality would come back, causing me to wonder when she finally would get over this. On those occasions, I was forced to remind myself of the reality of what I had done—that she was the victim, not me. She told me how I had destroyed the image she had of me as her knight in shining armor. Other times, I sensed her turmoil as she tried to forgive me.

I was required to do a full disclosure. I was obliged to do as told. The worst times were when I heard her sobbing in the bathroom with the door locked. I was frightened, ashamed, and felt dirty. I also feared she might never again be happy. During these difficult times, my support group stood by my side and gave me hope. They insisted that I focus on my shortcomings and that in time our marriage would heal. They were right. Today our marriage is stronger than we had ever thought possible. I never would have been able to muster up the courage to come clean without the help and support of others.

Whether an addict or not, we all need people to do for us what we cannot accomplish for ourselves. When I finally reached the point in life where I felt comfortable trusting others with my decision-making process, I began to share in their strength and hope. Even when I started to isolate from my friends in the groups I attended, they knew me well enough to bring me out of it. Gradually, I began to make mental notes of new solutions to my problems.

I have helped many people in their recovery. The closer we get, the more they place their trust in me. This trust allows me to point out the blind spots they are unable to see on their own. Blind spots are usually created by the warden, that bully who berates us with destructive childhood messages of fear. Many of these fears are manufactured to inhibit growth and happiness.

Written inventories are excellent tools to bring our inner thoughts and fears to the surface. In group, these are our homework assignments. At our group meetings, we read what we've written to the group. We ask for feedback. These reports help identify our natural assets, liabilities, strengths, and weaknesses. In time, written inventories help to separate the manufactured fears of childhood from our healthy fears that are necessary for our survival. A healthy fear would tell us to say no to drugs or to stop and look both ways before dashing across a street. When people let imagined fears govern their lives, they lose their integrity and become angry and resentful. The combination of written inventories and fellowship support help us process our fears in a healthy way.

Being aware of manufactured fears is only the beginning. Awareness must be followed by action. Good intentions are not enough. Healing does not stem from intentions, but from a persevering attitude which can propel us to action despite discomfort.

Chapter Eight: ACTION!

Victim thinking gives us permission to
avoid taking responsibility.

ഇരുന്ന

Healing involves much more than meets the eye. Before you can begin to heal, you need to overcome roadblocks, which are mostly of your own doing. As I became aware of the ways in which my childhood wounds and my inner voice affected my life, I began to understand that my victim thinking pushed people away. This thinking, compounded by my fear of trusting others, created a distorted view of life. As I gained clarity, I realized that I needed to assume responsibility for my own actions and that being a victim was not working. I also needed the guidance of others.

The Stakes Are Higher for People with Destructive Behaviors

People with very destructive behaviors have a more compelling need to rely on the power of the group. The actions they need to take are more critical, because the consequences of their actions are more life threatening to themselves and to those around them. I have discovered one of the best ways to help myself is to help other people. When I'm busy helping others, I put their needs first rather than focusing solely on myself. In giving to others, I receive more in return.

The deeper the childhood wounds, the greater the difficulty it will be to ask for help. Deeply wounded people tend to blame others without assuming any personal responsibility for their own problems. Their sense of personal responsibility is eclipsed by layers of self-loathing, false pride, and toxic shame. When newcomers first begin to attend our groups, it takes them time to fully understand the meaning of acceptance as it relates to their personal problems. As a group leader, I try to be the voice of acceptance for them. I urge them to keep coming back to group. In time, and after a lot of hard work, they can begin to free themselves from the fears and intrusive voices that have chained them to a life of isolation and regret.

One of the first things I do when a newcomer joins the group is to inquire why he or she needs help, and if they are willing to accept it when given. When trying to urge a newcomer to participate in group therapy, I begin by sharing the feelings and problems I had when I first came for help. I tell them about the warden, the guy who sits on my shoulder with a bat. I ask if they have a warden on their shoulder too, and what he tells them. When someone has a difficult childhood, they go through life with a feeling of defectiveness. When they experience failure, their past shame resurfaces in the present. Eventually, the failure takes on a bigger meaning and can represent how the person defines him- or herself. Of course, this message is encouraged by their warden.

I ask newcomers how they feel when someone disagrees with them. Do they shut down, believing they do not deserve to have their feelings heard? Or, do they rage at any opinion that doesn't agree with theirs? In the past, when I met with disagreement my feelings of defectiveness would resurface; I mistakenly thought that being right would make the pain go away. But, the only thing that went away was the people in my life. Whether a newcomer shuts down their emotions or lashes out in anger, neither way is healthy.

Learning to trust is a slow process, and it's OK to build it by taking tiny steps. Our darkest secrets are the most critical ones to expose. These secrets imprison a person to a life of toxic shame, adding fuel to our destructive thinking. My responsibility as a guide is to nurture sufficient trust so the newcomer to our group will allow me to be their new temporary decision maker. Dark secrets are like cancerous growths. If they are permitted to grow and metastasize, they will devastate a person's emotional well-being.

Positive feelings, on the other hand, are short-lived because the old voices return to haunt us. Our inner voice convinces us of our inadequacies; it becomes even more critical for me—as their guide—to stay close following any disclosure of secrets. Gary's story demonstrates the importance of disclosing our destructive secrets before healing can begin.

Gary

Gary is single and in his forties. According to Gary, "My childhood was shrouded in shame and secrecy. My father and I seldom spoke, and I was ashamed by his habit of walking around the house naked at times. I found this very humiliating. He was also so selfish that he would put a chain around the freezer so that no one would take any of his ice cream or desserts. My mother suffered from depression. As I got older I felt that even though she loved us, we were a bother to her more than anything else.

"At a very young age I became aware that I had an attraction to males. My mother caught me with someone and made me write a letter to my father explaining what I did. I had to read this letter aloud and the amount of shame was unbearable. I wanted to die. Ironically, my father, who was reading the paper at the time, said nothing. As I look back on it, I wish he would have gotten mad. At least it would have been a sign of emotion. In later years, I found out that my father was a cross-dresser and had many secrets of his own. As crazy as it sounds, I wanted his love anyway, but he never allowed this to happen. On occasion, I would ask him for money, but he always turned me down. I don't even think I needed the money. I just wanted something, anything, just a sign that I mattered. The strongest message I was given as a child was not to share your secrets—that the humiliation of doing so would be devastating. I turned to drugs and alcohol to kill the pain."

Gary tried Twelve Step meetings, but the fear of disclosing his sexuality kept him disconnected from the people in the group. Instead, he went to a therapist, who suggested Gary make a phone call to someone who he thought he could trust. Gary called me. Gary recalls, "I felt comfortable talking until I was asked about my childhood. When this happened, my anger would come to the surface. I eventually learned that my anger was the way I subconsciously tried to push people away. It was suggested I try to do some written inventories on my childhood wounds. I still got angry every time doing these inventories was suggested.

"I was told, 'You will never feel like doing them, so if you're waiting for that to happen, no progress will ever be made.' Eventually, I built enough faith and willingness to do what I was told. I hated to admit it, but I started to see how my fear of trusting others was manufactured from my childhood experiences. In time, I started to disclose stories about my past that I never thought I would share with anyone. Others were brought into my support system. I started to feel safer each time I had the courage to share my feelings with them."

It was difficult for Gary to open up about his fears and shame. But by bringing them to the surface, he was able to draw on the experience, strength, hope, and compassion of the group. He has slowly freed himself from those dark secrets of the past that had long kept him isolated in fear and desperation. This has also given him the willingness to go back to meetings, which in turn, have helped keep him from returning to his old destructive patterns.

The deeper the wounds, the greater our defenses that discourage us from hearing new information and insights about healing. New information requires us to look at our wounds instead of ignoring them. Old information is like an alarm system that sounds— *danger, danger, someone is trying to see who I am and I won't allow this under any circumstances.* Yet, there is a part of us that desperately wants to trust someone and feel protected and cared for. My cry was, *"Please help me. I'm in so much pain, but don't you dare come near me."* Building trust and closeness with someone who has never experienced intimacy can be the most beautiful experience to witness. If they have the willingness to keep reaching out, they will eventually expose a part of themselves that has always cried out for acceptance.

I helped a man who constantly tried to push me away by asking, "Why do you care about somebody like me?" He felt so worthless. Underneath his protective wall, he was begging for help and eventually found the courage to trust. There are times we can share our loving Higher Power with others who cannot find it on their own. One of the ways I share this gift is to let the person know they will never again be alone unless it is their choice to live a solitary life. What I cannot supply is the willingness to change. This they must find on their own.

The teacher of willingness is life itself, and we become willing students once we recognize that we can no longer live the way we had in the past. We must involve ourselves with others who are trying to improve their lives. The greater our participation, the more bonded we will feel with the group. These groups can be formed by a therapist, church, housewives, or any group of people who willing to adhere to the criteria and rules suggested here previously.

However, participation is mandatory. The decision to place phone calls to other members of the group is mandatory. Even if the person has nothing to talk about, he or she still is obligated to make phone calls. Gradually, the phone calls become easier as the comfort level increases in the members.

One common struggle we share as humans is our difficulty to admit defeat. This is because our society views defeat as weak. We were taught never to give up, but sometimes giving up allows us to seek help. At times, the sooner a person does this and admits defeat, the sooner he can begin to heal. By surrounding ourselves with the right people, we begin to stop some of the destructive habits and entitlements that have always hurt us.

I am grateful that on my journey I have established deep friendships with people of all faiths, sexual preferences, and walks of life. Some were brought up in an environment with a strong belief in a Higher Power. Yet they turned to addiction or other destructive actions to cope with life's problems. Defectiveness, unworthiness, shame, abandonment, and never feeling good enough are common threads. With these characteristics, it is easy to develop an inner voice that tells you how different you are from other people. If our care-givers manipulated or abused us in childhood in any way, we will carry this distrust into our adult lives. It affects all of our relationships with others.

The only reason I was able to trust others was because I realized that I could not stop my destructive actions on my own. What I found was even greater than merely staying sober. I discovered a freedom from my childhood wounds that was only possible when I became willing to permit others to do for me what I was incapable of doing for myself. One of the tools that I credit most for my growth is the written inventories included in this book on pages 99 and 111. These inventories allowed me to trust. The first written inventory focuses on the messages we receive as children. From these messages, we hear a voice that directs us toward inappropriate actions and destructive behaviors.

Displacement

According to Dr. Twerski's definition of displacement, "At any time, a person may come into contact with someone who occupies a position similar to that of a parent, perhaps an authority figure such as a teacher or boss. Since there is no guilt in feeling angry at one's teacher or boss, our subconscious mind allows our angry feelings to come out of storage and be directed at the teacher or boss. These feelings are *displaced* since neither the teacher nor the boss had done anything to warrant such feeling being directed toward them.

"Here we have a situation where this person feels angry at his teacher or boss with no justification. Although displaced anger at a boss is not as uncomfortable as anger directed toward a parent, it is nevertheless an uncomfortable feeling to be angry at someone for no good reason. The subconscious mind uses one of its other maneuvers, *rationalization,* to give the person logical-sounding reasons to justify his feelings. A person might say, 'Did you see how your teacher walked right by you, as if you didn't exist?' Or, 'Your teacher didn't show you adequate appreciation for the amount of work you did or the effort you made.' The subconscious mind is very clever in getting a person to believe what it wants him or her to believe."

The fact is, according to Dr. Twerski, you can go through life with distorted feelings about yourself and other people. These other people may be your spouse, parents, in-laws, siblings, children, employer, friends, and anyone else with whom you have a relationship. Dr. Twerski reminds us, "Your behavior toward them may be unpleasant, resulting in distress. You may think you know why you're behaving that way toward them, although your behavior is factually without foundation. They, in turn, may relate to you on the basis of your behavior. It is easy to see how many important relationships can be all messed up because of such misconceptions. If only we could free ourselves, think how much better life could be."

The following is an example of a written inventory. We complete inventories to make us aware of the ways our childhood caregivers have affected the relationships we now have as adults.

A Written Inventory

Who were your caregivers?	Messages received from those caregivers	Our inner voice created from the messages	The behaviors our inner voice commands us to do	What we need from our support system
1. Dad	From Dad: I wasn't good enough.	That I'm inadequate.	Isolation.	Help me renew trust in others.
2. Mom	From Mom: Her feelings mattered more than mine.	That I am not a good person unless I am pleasing others.	No one would like me if they discover who I really am.	
3. Priest	God's love was conditional.	Don't trust in others because they will unfairly judge you.		

Journaling is a way to explore thoughts and feeling while contemplating what action to take. As the person reveals what they have learned to others, he begins to connect the dots. For the first time he recognizes the fears he inherited from his childhood and how they led him to play a role in his adult life that helped him cope with his fears. As new, healthier voices take root, they rely less heavily on the old ones. The more we can challenge our old way of doing things, the more we can accept and strengthen our faith in ourselves and others.

When a person finishes his or her written inventories there will be enough evidence to demonstrate the reasons the person does not trust others in their life. I tell the person, "It is obvious why you would not want to trust the group, therapist, sponsor, or anyone else.

If trusting others resulted in such negative consequences, then why would you put any faith in a process you cannot control?" I ask each person what he or she needs from the group or me to help battle the destructive messages inside their heads. When members reveal those messages and inner voices to the group, they find they are not so unique. Others begin to share all the ways they can identify with the member. In time, the person will become aware of the ways these childhood inner voices are affecting relationships in the here and now.

One person who gained great insight from these written inventories was Ernie. Ernie never realized the damage caused by his resentment toward his father. He lost three jobs in two years and blamed it all on his bosses. In many ways, Ernie's written inventories brought him the self-awareness he needed to help him change.

Ernie

Ernie is thirty years old, married, and has three children. According to Ernie, "When I was young, my authority figure was my father. My dad's intended message was that his children were a status symbol and not worthy in their own rights. A successful person had lots of money, a big house, a nice car, children who listen, and community status. Dad had all these things, and my siblings and I were just part of his success.

"Dad worked long hours and rarely took time to spend with us. Much of his free time was devoted to community-related activities. Throughout my entire childhood, my dad took me to a total of one baseball game. He never taught me to play ball, nor did he just hang out with me. His other activities were more important.

"When Dad was around, he tended to be very strict and had a short fuse. At our Shabbat table, if I were to move around, speak too loudly, or do anything that my dad felt out of place, he would yell at me. He held us to a very high and probably impossible standard of behavior. Children were to be seen and not heard."

Ernie's father had an insult for every occasion. Ernie recalls, "His idea of interaction was to insult his kids. We learned to give as well as take, but God help us if we ever got the better of him in one of his tirades. If that happened, we were being insulting and disrespectful to our father, a major no-no, and subject to punishment. It seemed he didn't care about our feelings, and we were not allowed to fight back or defend ourselves against his authority.

"My dad did not have a problem expressing his disapproval, and he was always very blunt. 'You look like shit,' was the typical criticism referring to our state of dress. 'You're an idiot and have no idea what you're talking about, so shut up,' was the usual remark. He also used to say these things in front of other people, which made us feel worthless."

As an adult, Ernie realized how he used anger as a weapon, especially toward his wife. He says, "If I'm not acting out in anger, then I'm isolating. I also get angry at my kids for not behaving. I disconnect from those who can punish me, especially my wife. When I see my wife as an authoritative figure, I cut myself off from her. If I disconnect then she can't touch me. I'm so afraid of feeling worthless or ignored that when this feeling comes up I react with anger. This also creates a voice inside me that says I must be right all the time and when others disagree I become very defensive.

"Today, with the help of others, I've learned to take a step back from my old reactions of anger and rage and instead examine myself before the rage happens. I am learning how being gentle with myself and empathetic toward my wife can help me move away from rage. But in order to practice that gentleness and empathy, I need awareness and a course of action that I must take to short-circuit that process before it occurs. I also have learned to confront many issues that I have with my father, including repressed anger, sadness, fear, and my lack of self-worth."

Some people were so fearful of their childhood caregivers that they carried this fear into their adult life. This was the case with Ernie. Even therapists and guides can be targets of his anger. Ernie has a difficult time with change and accepting guidance, and he is frequently critical of new ideas. This created unmanageability in his life and stopped him from reaching out for help because he was so harshly judged in childhood.

In deeply wounded families, our mistakes are often used as weapons against each other. This was the case with Ernie. Ernie had the desire to punish himself for his mistakes by not permitting compassion into his belief system. As our relationship evolved, he began to make room in his life for kindness and tolerance, both for himself and for others. Inventories helped Ernie realize how he is passing on his distorted mindset to his offspring. They also helped him discover how much joy he gets from the role of victim, especially when it comes to his father. Anger toward his father is part of his natural fiber, but it also has served another purpose. First, anger protected him from the need to tell his father how he truly feels; anger also has allowed him to deny his own grief that was covered over with layer upon layer of anger. Eventually, Ernie found the courage to tell his father how it felt to be a little kid and face that ten-foot giant called Dad. By saying no to the voice inside his head, Ernie has slowly learned to share these fears and release himself from the wounds of the past.

Joining a Support Group

We have established the importance of trust and of learning how to rely less on ourselves and to rely more on others. In the beginning of my healing process, I had to have a Higher Power with "skin," such as a therapist or a support group.

A support group can be two or more individuals, which lend support to each other. A group can meet in a church, school, or in someone's house. A group must choose a leader to enforce the group guidelines. As the group evolves, it will take on a life of its own with its peaks and valleys. Start the meeting by discussing each member's goals and the obstacles that block these goals. Goals can range from increasing one's intimacy with family members to finding the courage to say no to parents or others. Goals can include asking your boss for a raise or finding a new job altogether.

Eventually, through the guidance of my support group, I found a spiritual power. It's hard to find a spiritual power when you feel like a victim. Victim thinking leaves little room for gratitude, and gratitude is needed to find a Higher Power. I must constantly remind myself that I could be alone, in jail, divorced, sick, or dead. Simply put, I am grateful for what I have rather than what I don't have. It could be worse.

Getting the Most from a Support Group

Through my own experience, I have found twelve ways to help you get the most out of support groups and help free yourself from victim thinking. The more willing you are to try helpful hints like the ones listed below, the better chance you have to stay away from being a victim and self-righteous. Destructive actions are deadly, creating a spiritual death that separates the person from everyone else in his life. Changing your behavior presents a day-to-day challenge. To help you be more successful in your group therapy, consider the following suggestions.

- *When anger strikes, take a time out.* Once anger takes control it becomes difficult to surrender. Seek guidance and strength from your support group, from friends, or from other sources that bring enjoyment to your life. The sooner you can do this, the easier it becomes to change old patterns of behavior. Be careful not to seek those that support the Warden's destructive messages.

- *Phone someone you trust in your support/accountability group when you are angry.* Make sure it is someone who will slowly guide the conversation to a healthy solution. The guide must direct you away from self-pity or entitlement.

- *Before approaching a person who angers you, discuss the problem first with your support group.* Group members can discuss a better way to communicate how you feel in a healthy way.

- *Talk to your group about your destructive inner voice.* Don't let your actions follow the voice. Your group will help you find healthy solutions for your problems.

- *Be direct.* Ask your group for courage and strength when your fears try to shut you down. Saying no to others can create unhealthy guilt. On the other hand, if you say "Yes" when you want to say "No," then the victim thinking starts to build again. The better choice is speaking with integrity.

- *Recite daily affirmations to increase self-esteem.* These affirmations are more powerful if they are done in front of a mirror. I had to say to myself that I deserved to be loved even if I didn't feel it inside. I did this every morning no matter how difficult or uncomfortable it was for me.

- *Tell your partner your struggles.* It may be uncomfortable, but this communication can increase intimacy between you and your partner. Learn to listen to your partner. To get the best results, couples should make the commitment to be honest with each other and to share their feelings in a safe way.

- *As parents, commit to sharing some of your challenges with your children.* By doing this, you can build a new belief system, one that enables your children to learn that it's all right to ask for help.

- *Keep your feet where they should be—not where they can get you into trouble.* This advice is especially important for recovering addicts.

- *Check in with your partner.* Share your feelings in scheduled get-togethers during the week. As you start to experience new feelings with your partner, you can share these feelings with your support group if needed. This enables everyone in the group to learn and grow from each others' experiences.

- *Admit when you are wrong as soon as possible.* If you aren't open about your mistakes, your thinking might naturally gravitate toward blaming the other person.

- *In addition to group, consider seeking the help from a qualified therapist.*

Doing the Next Right Thing

In healing, we talk about doing the next right thing. Unfortunately, the next right thing is not always the most comfortable thing to do. Often the right thing requires that you step out of your comfort zone. Making a connection with your support group is the right thing, but may not be comfortable because you have grown more at ease being isolated. When ruled by self-hatred and destructive behaviors, the only words a person is capable of absorbing are words that reinforce his worthlessness. If a person goes back to his destructive behaviors or is involved in relationships he is ashamed of, he will avoid the healthy people in his life. Being around healthy people causes his shame. He will only seek healthy people when he reaches utter despair.

Those who were judged in childhood will have a more difficult time feeling safe when expressing their shortcomings or mistakes to others. Sometimes the only option left is to leave a door open for them to call on when they decide to end their isolation. I can't help anyone battle their destructive inner voice unless they allow me to join the fight. When they are ready, I can guide them through the shame they are bound to feel upon coming back to their group. It does not matter how many times they come back, as long as they keep coming back.

People who are severely wounded do not have healthy boundaries. They either blame others for their troubles or make themselves responsible for everyone else's shortcomings. It is hard for them to see the gray area because victim thinking sees only black or white.

The Power of Personal Inventories

The first set of personal inventories helped us understand how early childhood messages created inner voices that affected our belief system as adults. The second inventory must be calculated regularly to help us cope with the daily occurrences of our lives and to recognize the distorted way we view ourselves. As our self-perception becomes less distorted, we become more accepting of others, which eventually decreases the victim thinking that has harmed us until now.

Personal inventories are an effective tool to gain valuable personal insight. When a flood of old information overwhelms you, it distorts your perceptions about yourself and the world around you. Taking a personal inventory at this stage helps to restore your balance by looking at your role in the incident, rather than viewing yourself as the victim. You begin to gain a better perspective on how your thinking has to change, rather than how others need to change. In one of my first inventories, I had so much denial that I could not see my responsibility in anything. I had a problem saying no to people, so I thought every problem I had was the other person's fault. I didn't realize that this was how I set myself up to be a victim. In reality I did not have the courage to say no because my inner voice made me feel like a bad person if I didn't make others happy. When this happened, I was angry that people took advantage of me. In reality, it was my fault for letting them take advantage of me. I also thought that I was a great husband, because I never complained. In reality, I was shutting down because I had no self-worth. These things became clear as I continued my written inventories.

Each member of the group must share his inventories with other members so we can discuss our experiences together. This is important because support groups can point out our blind spots. It allows us to recognize our victim thinking before we start to act on it. It also guides us toward a healthy solution and away from self-righteous thoughts. When we start to include inventories as part of our daily discipline, a healthy change in our thinking emerges. Instead of setting ourselves apart from the world and wallowing in self-pity, we start to examine our role in life. This allows us to become more accepting of others and to find forgiveness.

Celebrate Victories

People with troubled childhoods do not take the time to celebrate their victories in life. Rather than acknowledging progress, the person will immediately move to another dilemma. For example, when I did something constructive in my life or had a sense of gratitude, it was important to share these experiences with my support group. The accomplishment of one group member can bring hope to other members.

Beware of Complacency

Whenever I am introduced to something new, such as a self-help tool, my immediate reaction is to put up resistance, even if I know that it is the right thing to do. I have learned that if the suggestion is coming from a reliable source, it's best to do what I am told and guard against complacency. Many people who reach the point of taking a personal inventory develop a certain level of peace. They have started to feel better about themselves, and this feeling filters into their personal relationships. Then suddenly, false pride finds a crack in the armor and they feel they deserve a break from doing the things that have improved their lives. The cycle returns: first complacency, then isolation, then self-pity, and finally entitlement. Even those who have stayed away from their destructive ways for years underestimate the power of their inner voice and their victim thinking and eventual isolation. Isolation always provided a comfort zone for me.

Inventories serve as an important tool to keep you in the present, which increases the likelihood you will not go back to your old ways. There are no guarantees, but those who do inventories regularly will grow in self-awareness and acceptance of others. Inventories also help to form healthy boundaries in our relationships, so we can clearly see where our responsibility begins and ends. In the beginning, doing inventories is bothersome, but like other disciplines, once you are in the habit of doing them, you've won half the battle. The reward is the freedom that comes when other people can no longer control your life.

Another problem many people face is their own negative attitude. When I detect such a defeatist attitude, I tell them, "Your best thinking got you here." This is why I suggest they take their thinking out of the equation. I remind them that this takes time and patience. After all, they didn't get this way overnight. Whether it is praying, calling people, or taking an inventory, these processes take time before beliefs begin to change.

Before beginning your personal inventory, here are a few suggestions to get you started. All of these actions appear simple to do, but may be blocked by flawed thinking.

- *The habit of taking a personal inventory is like the habit of praying.* Do it on a consistent basis and not just when you are in trouble or when the spirit moves you. Do not wait until you feel like doing your inventories, as this feeling may never come. Just do it.

- *An inventory helps you find out more about the distorted thinking that creates the destructive behavior.* It also builds awareness about wounds that have influenced your life as an adult. Patterns eventually develop in these inventories so you can see how your victim thinking has affected your life.

- *Written inventories work more efficiently if completed for fifteen to thirty minutes a night, instead of three hours once a week.* It keeps the mind alert to the dynamics of daily thinking.

- *With time, inventories should bring acceptance and awareness of the ways our inner voice has influenced adult behaviors.* Eventually, the goal is to feel comfortable in our own skin, rather than carrying the shame-filled baggage of our childhood wounds.

Written Inventories

When I started my inventory, it was like a jigsaw puzzle. I could only conclude that I was on one end of the spectrum while everyone else was on the other. I placed the blame on everyone else for my problems. But after taking an inventory for a period of time, I began to better understand my role and how I allowed victim thinking and self-righteousness to influence my outlook on my relationships and the world.

Many people I have worked with, especially those with successful careers, are trapped in denial. They can recognize neither their victim mentality nor the warden sitting on their shoulders. Because they are successful, it is often difficult for them to accept the possibility that they can be engaged in victim thinking. The likelihood that they covered this up by becoming overachievers is a mystery to them. Even though they often struggle with hopelessness and sometimes despair, they still don't believe that something has gone awry. This is where the inventories come to the rescue. This is where they can discover that either directly or indirectly they can set up themselves or others for unrealistic expectations. This can trigger a downward spiral that often leads to drugs, alcohol, working compulsively, or some other form of destructive entitlement.

Taking an Inventory

An inventory is a personal self-examination where we record our thought process on paper. This enables us to see a clearer picture of the ways our thinking affects our relationships. As we do inventories, we begin to see patterns developing that make our part in the problem more distinguishable. By discussing these inventories with others, our wounds and defects are brought to the light, which brings healing and growth into our relationships. The first column of the inventory lists the names of persons or institutions that harmed us or did something to strike a raw nerve or open an old wound. The second column describes the nature of the incident. In this column, the individual must keep his writing to a minimum. It is tempting to be overly detailed in writing about the details of the situation. The goal here is to avoid self-righteousness—which keeps us from being in touch with our emotional wounds. The third column lists our initial reaction to the incident. The fourth column describes the old wound that has been reopened by the incident and the cause of our overreaction. It encompasses the character defects and wounds which influence our perceptions of the world. How have we let our childhood wounds set ourselves up to become victims, when the reality is that we are often the aggressors?

If the wounded person expects too much of another, then he will spend his life being victimized by that person. This makes acceptance of others impossible. Unless these wounds and voices are exposed, we will not find freedom from the power others have over us. Our feelings of defectiveness ultimately influence the way we respond to the incident. These childhood injuries make the person a prisoner to a defective belief system.

The wound must be named and the voice that comes from this injury must be brought into the inventory in column four. Were any unfair expectations set up that created predetermined resentments? Did the person judge herself or others too rigidly in the situation? Were there any feelings of defectiveness which might have been similar to those that were felt as children? Did the person feel invisible or ignored in any area, as in childhood? The person might have been too caught up in the right and wrong of the situation, which would feed into her belief that she had to be right in order to feel good inside. Maybe the person was too selfish in the demands she made of others. These people might not have been able to give the person what she needed at the time because they had their own needs or problems to deal with. Was the person caretaking to the point that she felt manipulated and used? Did she say how she felt and was she completely honest? All of these old beliefs and coping strategies, which were protecting the individual's wounds, had to affect the way the person viewed the story. This third column is where the individual brings in her support group, if needed, to find out where one's blind spots are. In the beginning, it is difficult to see the migration into victimhood and self-righteousness. This is why a support group is essential for directing the person away from negative thinking.

The fifth column shows us that we have a choice; we can be more accepting and forgiving than our initial reaction. We also played a role in the initial incident that triggered our anger, and we are not innocent victims deserving of pity. We are learning to give or to ask for forgiveness, which is what finally releases us from the pain of our childhood wounds. This starts to change our mode of thinking from self-centered to gratitude centered. We develop gratitude for the way things are rather than for the way we want them to be. Gratitude will always be the water that extinguishes the flames of victim thinking.

Instead of focusing on how others harm us, we begin to see the bigger picture—that everyone has problems and everyone is not out to get us. We no longer need to have their problems own us. After awhile, these written inventories lay the groundwork for building healthy boundaries. You will soon discover the insanity of doing the same things repeatedly and expecting different results. You will also discover the healing power of acceptance and forgiveness as the only way to release yourself from the grip that our inner voice and others have over us.

Review the sample inventory below. Then do your own inventory in the space provided. A blank example of this inventory is included in Appendix A on page 151. You may want to make photocopies of the inventories for your personal use.

The Aggressor	The incident	My initial reaction, aided by the Warden's voice	Old fears and wounds re-opened by event	A more mature & compassionate reaction that addresses my role in the incident
My wife	Criticized me for my past infidelity	Anger for dredging up the past	Abandonment, insecurity & inadequacy	Showing kindness empathy and compassion
My children	They don't help out around the house	Anger for not helping	That I'm a failure as a father	To establish boundaries and consequences
My mother	My difficulty in saying no	Anger and guilt	Fear of manipulation	No longer have to carry her shame
God	For letting my father die	I felt like a victim	Fear of abandonment	Your will, not mine, be done
Me	Making a mistake	Impatience & anger	Feeling inadequate	Feeling self-compassion

The Aggressor	The incident	My initial reaction, aided by the Warden's voice	Old fears and wounds re-opened by event	A more mature & compassionate reaction that addresses my role in the incident

After your written inventories are completed, read them
to your support group or sponsor and talk about what happened
to trigger your anger or other feelings. Explore if you felt *defective,
unworthy, humiliated and invisible,* or *abandoned.*

The inventory can be a great problem-solving tool, especially
regarding conflict resolution with family members. It has helped me
resolve problems I have had with my mother and my brothers by
allowing me to see how much emphasis I put on *being right* instead
of *feeling connected* or close to them. Some parents unknowingly pit
siblings against each other. All that a parent needs to do is imply that
one child should act more like the other one to get positive attention.
It isn't surprising when siblings give more compassion to strangers
than they do to each other. When I get mad at my siblings, my victim
thinking takes me right into self-righteousness. It is more comfortable
to focus on their shortcomings than my own. The problem is, all of
my energy is focused on being right, which leaves little room for
compassion. Inventories have taught me that since I don't walk in
other people's shoes, I have no right to judge them.

In my childhood, everyone wanted to be right, producing a
climate where no one felt safe enough to admit his or her wrongs.
The pain of exposing any failure to other members of the family would
be catastrophic, so everyone wore a false mask. As I healed internally,
I found myself praying for humility and the courage to allow my
family members to see who I am and to surrender the outcome of what
might happen afterward.

I was given a great opportunity two years ago. One of my
brothers went into a treatment center for his addictions. I wanted so
desperately to share my own experiences, strengths, and hopes with
him, but the rehabilitation center did not allow visitors. I also wanted
to ask him for forgiveness over how I treated him when we were
younger. I had a lot of anger as a child, and, regrettably, I took some
of my anger out on two of my three siblings. I asked him to let me
know if I hurt him in ways I wasn't aware of. I also shared my own
experiences, and how afraid I was as a child and as an adult. I was
the oldest and always considered the strong, successful one. When he
got out of treatment, we had several long, emotional conversations.

Because we had never shared such intimacy, I had never felt closer to him. Through our discussions, he began to share his childhood stories. He told me how he would come into my room at night and sleep at the end of my bed because he felt so afraid. He also told me that I was a source of protection for him, shielding him from the insecurity in our house. I was so caught up in my own survival that I never realized this, or had any empathy for my brother as a child. I felt sorry I could not be there, and told him how scary it must have been for him.

My brother's wife told me my letter freed him from his guilt. By sharing my weaknesses, he found more compassion for his own shortcomings. By combining the knowledge I gained in my inventory work with the strength I received from my support group, I allowed my brother to see who I really am. I found the courage to be vulnerable and let go of the outcome, which the warden tried to sabotage in his efforts to create a bad ending to a wonderful story. Through these tools, we have a better relationship today than ever before.

An inventory allows me to see clearly the personal struggle going on between my old belief system and my new belief system. An inventory also allows me to achieve greater self-awareness. It affords me the opportunity to recognize how people in my life needed me more than I needed them; to see how I was always playing caretaker instead of caring for myself. As I began to grow in awareness, it became clear that some of my greatest career strengths were also my greatest obstacles to personal growth. The self-reliance and willpower that led to my financial success weren't helpful qualities when it came to internal growth. This is why it is so important to find self-acceptance, because my strengths in one area are my weaknesses in another.

Self-Reliance

Relying on myself was an essential part of my business success. I had to do things my way, which in many instances resulted in success. In my healing process, my self-reliance was killing me. It constantly put me on the same path of destruction. When I started to rely more on others, I eliminated the false notion that everything would only work out if I was in total control.

Willpower

Willpower is another great quality for survival and success in business. I never gave up on anything. During my healing process, I reached a point where I had to learn to give up doing things my way and admit defeat, because my way only brought pain and dissatisfaction. By refusing to surrender my willpower, I continued to run into the same wall. When I finally surrendered my willpower, I discovered new solutions to my problems.

I also began to see how my real and manufactured fears were obscuring my outlook on life. Some fears were healthy and kept me from taking harmful actions, but the fears manufactured by the warden had to be turned over to my support group. The amount of time I spent worrying about the future left me with little energy to take care of present matters. At other times, I spent too much time on the past, allowing the pain of childhood to predict my future. This prison sentence was determined by my injured past.

Finally, these written inventories allowed me to see that pain is a prerequisite for growth. I have heard it said, *If it feels bad it doesn't always mean it is bad, and if it feels good it doesn't always mean it is good.* I started to believe that I did not have to know what the future would hold in order to feel safe. Many changes in my thinking are the result of doing an inventory, staying away from bad behaviors, having a trusted support group, and developing a relationship with a loving, protecting Higher Power.

A part of me resisted changes. There were times when I fought going to a therapist, going to a group, making phone calls, or doing personal inventories. I did not notice the improvement at first, as the warden tried to hide my growth, reemphasizing that I did not deserve peace in my life. My life used to be filled with chaos and insanity. If everything was in total disarray, I had little time to focus on my own difficulties and shortcomings. I was used to playing the victim and blaming my problems on everyone else. My support group had to remind me of my growth, because I was unable to see it for myself.

The same thing happens with the people I help. I see the growth in them long before they see it in themselves. When old wounds are exposed, there will be pain as well. Facing these childhood injustices takes courage. Sometimes I remind them of where they are today compared to where they were. They may not be where they want to be, but they are certainly moving in the right direction. As they start to express themselves, instead of shutting down, they begin to expose their feelings of pain and isolation. When I help someone whose spouse's name keeps coming up in their written inventories, I try to find out what the person is really afraid of. Usually anger masks their fears, and their fear covers their emotional wounds. Eventually, through the written inventories, their fear will be exposed. The next step is to communicate these fears without resorting to anger. It is more productive for someone to talk about their *feelings* of fears, rather than their *objects* of anger. I use another exercise when a spouse's name is continually repeated in the inventory. This exercise is in the form of a balance sheet. On one side, I suggest they list the harms they have inflicted on their spouse, and on the other side list the harms their spouse has inflicted on them. Comparing harms on paper is a valuable way to reduce victim thinking and self-righteousness.

Suggestions for Struggling Couples

True intimacy is not possible with an active addiction going on in the relationship. Addictions nullify intimacy, because the addict will always choose addiction first. Healthy emotional connections will never be achieved with the addiction sitting between the partners.

Sobriety must always be the priority to the recovering addict. However, if someone has achieved long-term sobriety but is still going to Twelve Step meetings almost every day—at the expense of the relationships in his or her life—then this must be looked at. The fear of intimacy can be so powerful and insidious that even Twelve Step meetings can be subconsciously used as a way to avoid intimacy with a spouse and children.

Sometimes couples need to separate from each other for a period of time in order to clarify what needs fixing in their relationship. Some people are unwilling or unable to look at themselves unless this happens. If the relationship is characterized by blaming one another for its demise, self-righteous anger is difficult to surrender while living under the same roof. Each partner may see his or her spouse as the single problem in the marriage. If each spouse feels like a victim, neither will have the ability to listen to the needs of the other. Separation might be the only way of viewing his or her issues without the distractions of the partner. This offers the opportunity to connect with people who have walked through similar problems and found healthy solutions. With the help of therapists, groups, or some other support network, the person may look at the baggage he or she brought into the relationship without also looking into the partner's suitcase. Sometimes when there are difficulties in a marriage the spouse has to let go for the time being. This does not mean giving up on the relationship; it means working on one's own stuff and leaving the spouse's stuff alone for awhile.

Guidelines for Forming a Support Group

Perhaps you are interested in forming a support group. If so, let's start with the word *support*. Support can mean to hold up, reinforce, or sustain others who are experiencing trials or problems. A support group can be two or more individuals who lend support or reinforcement to the members. A group can meet in a church, school, or someone's house.

Everyone can benefit from a support group. With the help of others, we can feel strengthened to accomplish tasks that might otherwise be impossible to tackle alone. Groups are comprised of people from all walks of life, with the common denominator that all must be willing to unmask their feelings in a group situation. There will always be fear of the unknown when a new group starts.

A group must choose a leader to enforce the guidelines suggested in this book. As the group evolves, it will take on a life of its own with its peaks and valleys. It is imperative that the guidelines in this book are adhered to so healthy boundaries are in place. The meeting can begin by discussing each other's goals and the obstacles that block these goals. Usually your warden will be there to magnify any of your fears or uncertainties.

Goals for the group can range from increasing one's intimacy with family to finding the courage to say no to parents or others.

Goals can include asking your boss for a raise or finding a new job. Even finding support to clean one's house can be a goal brought up in group. Whatever the goal is, the support of others can help you free yourself from the warden's commands. It takes time to trust others and find the courage to act in our own best interests.

In order to run an effective group, it must adhere to certain principles to prevent it from becoming a social atmosphere. The rules for forming a group follow.

Trust and Safety

The most important elements of a support group are trust and anonymity. Whatever is shared must not be discussed with anyone outside the group. One of the ways support group members bond is by sharing their darkest secrets. Sharing painful experiences means the person has to be vulnerable to others, which takes a great deal of courage. In many instances the experiences that they are reluctant to share are the ones that truly help identify and define them as belonging to the group. In contrast, keeping secrets or sharing them selectively is harmful to the group, because they form a barrier between those who are in on the secret and those who are not.

Talk about Your Life Challenges

Each member should discuss his or her challenges in life; for example, a troubled relationship is a raw nerve for many of us. There is a shared identification in our challenges in life, which creates unity within the group and eventually contributes to personal growth among the members. It is helpful to share feelings of anger, defectiveness, inferiority, or invisibility, even though it is difficult to do at the beginning. However, you will find that once you eventually disclose these feelings, others will share their own experiences, strength, and hope, which further increase each member's connection with the group. Talking about each other's warden is a way to bring group unity. Remember, it is important to talk about the things that you do not feel like talking about.

Helping Others Feel Accepted

The group depends and thrives on mutual support. Each member should enjoy the acceptance of the group to help them overcome their daily struggles. Mutual compassion is also important since it helps validate each person's membership in the group. Asking for and giving help will build the unity of the group.

Reaching Out

The commitment to phoning each other is important. If a member faces a difficult challenge, a phone call can make all the difference in the world. Each member depends on the power of the group to help him or her face and overcome fears. An example is confronting a spouse, a parent, or a boss when you don't have the nerve. We all suffer from our own demons, but learning to face them so they don't hold us back is critical. A support group can empower us to face these difficulties head on, then move on. The next plateau will have a new set of challenges that can be shared, and from which all can benefit. Phone calls to a trusted individual help to reduce anger while fostering acceptance of the situation. The key is to give ourselves permission to quit doing things our own way and to seek the guidance of others. A phone call by the members of the group, before and after a difficult task, can make a tremendous difference to the individual.

Talk about Solutions

Healthy feedback builds confidence and can direct people away from self-righteousness and resentments. The goal is to pave the way for acceptance and forgiveness.

Allow Your Voice to Be Heard

Wounds inflicted early in life can remain tender. We protect these wounds by being oversensitive or avoiding conflict, but in the process we also avoid standing up for our own convictions. If we grew up feeling invisible as children, we may exhibit similar behavior in the group. This type of distorted thinking must be rooted out. You must commit to sharing whatever is bothering you; otherwise, those secrets will continue to fester. Each group session is a process that establishes accountability, where each group member holds him- or herself accountable to another with the goal to not resort to old ways of thinking. The function of the group is to empower its members to voice their innermost thoughts and problems.

In the first few sessions the members can discuss the ways they identify with each other or feel different from one another. Confrontation is also healthy for the group as long as it is done in a nonjudgmental way. When the members have healthy confrontation, using "I" statements and avoiding judgments allow their feelings to surface. Disagreements are a part of life and group dynamics. At any time, a member can say they do not want feedback and this request must be honored.

When a member feels stuck and is afraid to share, they can be asked to complete the sentence, "I am afraid of (name the situation)." By putting fears into words, this may be a way of starting the member's engine.

Bottling up feelings is a sure way to ignite your resentment, which can occur when one member feels less important than the others in the group. By bringing fears to the surface, the member builds integrity, knowing that he or she did not let their fears shut them down. Also, by expressing these fears and angers, the member can release some of the pain harbored inside. When the member finally breaks through his or her protective shell, he or she experiences a new sense of freedom, a personal victory previously unknown.

The group process brings unforeseen opportunities. At times a member could see their parents' characteristics in another member. They may also recognize behaviors in other members that resemble their children, siblings, fellow workers, or employers. Therefore, a support group can become a training session where members can improve the relationships in their lives while in the safety of the group setting.

The more the members become comfortable with each other, the more they will pull away from discussing the details of their past experiences and lean toward discussing the feelings of the present.

Eventually the members will take the lessons and new techniques they learn in group and apply them to the outside world.

Chapter Nine: Old Beliefs Versus New Beliefs

*A war can exist between the warden and a person's new belief system,
but as the person follows the actions suggested by their guides and support
group, the balance of power slowly shifts away from the warden.*

ℰℭ

The warden may be quiet for a while, but if we don't maintain
our new behaviors his voice will come back to sabotage our happiness.
Even when our lives improve, the warden sits in the background
waiting to mess up the situation. I have received calls from those
who have made great strides in their lives. They have found sobriety,
are back with their spouses, are building better relationships with
their children, and have improved their working environment.
Nevertheless, they start to sabotage their progress by pushing people
away with anger again. When love and closeness grow, so does the
fear of intimacy. As fear grows, we are reminded again that we don't
deserve happiness. This is why we mess up the situation for no
apparent reason. Sometimes our spouse will do the same. When we
take a step back in our lives, instead of beating ourselves up, we can
use these experiences to heighten our awareness and make better
choices in the future. We also gain a greater respect for the warden's
power, and that respect increases our willingness to maintain the
healthy connections in our lives.

My father ingrained in me that *your occupation defines who you
are.* This became part of my belief system. In the days my father acted
out his addictions, he believed that his business was the only thing
that he could depend on. His philosophy was that people would come
and go, but his business would always be there for him.

I was troubled when I had to lay off people; I felt that I let
them down. As the warden's voice increased in volume, I neglected to
talk to my support group about it. I was setting myself up again as the

victim. Eventually I returned to my therapist, who reminded me of the danger in listening to this voice and not talking about it with others. Rather than face my problems squarely and share them with others, I suppressed the pain and ignored the wounds. I had to admit that part of me was angry over business failures. I felt like a failure. Once I started to do my written inventories again, I began to lose the victim thinking and was able to turn down the warden's volume. By accepting the way things were, instead of fighting them, I eventually developed a sense of gratitude. I also started to accept that things change and that I had another calling in life—to help those that needed help.

To help show the differences between new and old beliefs, I compare two thought processes in the following table. The first column lists the negative voices and distorted belief system from the past. This thinking is self-centered, implying that new information will not work and only result in more difficulty. The second column identifies a thought process that is open to new beliefs and attitudes. It is people centric, embraces patience, and avoids immediate gratification. As we allow newer information into our belief system, we start to build integrity and self-esteem. We begin to feel that we deserve happiness.

The Old Voice (The Warden)	New Inner Voices
No one can do for me what I can do for myself.	My best thinking brought isolation and loneliness into my life. Now I can try open mindedness
People aren't safe; they will hurt me.	The people in my life today are not the same people I grew up with.
Why bother to share my feelings with my wife? If she really cared she would know what I'm thinking.	My part is to share my feelings with my wife in a safe way and let go of the outcome.
I don't need any more therapy, groups, or meetings.	I need people to do for me what I can't do for myself.
It is hopeless. I'll never get better.	Think about all the ways my life has gotten better when I allow people into it.
I'm afraid things won't work out the way I want them to so I think I must control it.	I need to find faith in people who truly care for me. I can allow myself to let them help me make my decisions in life.

The Old Voice (The Warden)	New Inner Voices
I want what I want when I want it.	What can I do for someone else without expecting something in return? Learn to be patient.
Everything happens to me. I just have bad luck and it's not fair.	What part did I play in the situations that happened today?
I do not deserve happiness.	I deserve to be happy.
I cannot say no to people. Saying no would make them think less of me, and that would be painful.	When I say no to someone, it causes pain. Find other people who I trust who can guide me through this pain.
Everyone should think the way I want them to; after all, I have to always prove I'm right.	I do not have to be right; instead, I can find closeness by listening to the feelings of others.
I have a sense of self-righteousness; I'm better than him. Look what he's done.	Help me to see that person with the same understanding and compassion I want from others.
The more money I make, the happier I will be.	Remember my past. Money never fixed my wounds before, and it won't now.
I don't deserve happiness.	If I cannot find a voice of compassion within me, then I will find this kindness from my support system.
If I discipline my kids, I will lose their love.	If I feel like a bad parent let me seek the support of others to help me through this pain.
Don't ever share fear or emotion because this is a sign of weakness.	Let people see my weakness as a part of who I really am.
I'm afraid of asking questions because people will think I'm stupid.	Help me accept myself exactly as I am. I am not perfect.
I can't trust a spiritual power, because I've already been judged as a bad person.	A loving spiritual power will accept all of me, the good and bad.
I am not good enough to write this book. Who do I think I am?	Help me find the courage from my support system to share my experiences and hopes with others and let go of all the fears that will try to stop me from moving forward.

Old information from childhood was not intended to hurt us, but this was the only information our caregivers had at that time. Without the willingness to let new information into our thinking, it becomes difficult to change. There is still an internal collision going on between the two belief systems trying to control our thinking and dictate our actions. We should reach out the most when it becomes the most difficult. Isolation becomes the warden's greatest weapon, and gratitude is the warden's greatest nemesis.

As we begin the step of maintenance in our lives we begin to feel free from the chains of the old behaviors. As our belief system changes we start to see the distorted reality from the past. We become aware of patterns in our thinking that were driven by self-centered fear. Our new belief system slowly convinces us that we are good people who deserve to be happy. The more we feel that we deserve happiness, the less likely we will do things to sabotage this belief. Peace of mind comes from *accepting* certain things in life rather than *expecting* them.

By changing our view of reality, we also change our behavior. We find ourselves reacting far less to outside circumstances.

As we heal and grow emotionally, we lose self-centeredness. However, if we are too busy protecting our wounds and only thinking of self-survival, it leaves little room for anyone else. When we start to heal, the people we love get the attention they deserve. Sometimes others see the change in us before we do. We don't want to be a slave to our addictions or a slave to what other people think of us anymore. The more we grow, the more our integrity builds. We find ourselves less concerned over other people's actions. All of these actions become easier as we start to feel comfortable in our own skin for the first time. We can't forget about our past, but we don't have to let the past have a negative effect on our lives today.

The trust I have placed in people has helped me the most. Even with spiritual growth, I still need guides to continue my healing. There are many wonderful institutions that offer all kinds of support to people who suffer from a wounded past. Bookstores are full of self-help literature that fosters self-awareness. All these things are helpful, but self-knowledge is not enough to battle the warden in all of us. Actions and beliefs are so ingrained, whether harmful or not, that change occurs only when we accept three important elements in our lives: awareness, positive actions, and maintenance.

The first essential is *awareness*. It is essential to become aware of the ways our old belief system created this warden, which fought anything that disagreed with it. Even though this guy with the bat on our shoulder was hurting us, we still listened to every command. If the caregivers in our childhood hindered us from trusting others, the rebirth of trust in our lives is the stepping stone to healing our past. This is the reason any self-help procedure must be reinforced with a support system of trusting people.

The second essential involves the *positive actions* we need to incorporate into our daily affairs. If we stick to the disciplines in this book, we can slowly change our old belief system. But the warden will not go away without a fight.

This is why we need the third essential, *maintenance*. If we don't keep ourselves connected to our support groups and do the written inventories the warden's voice will get louder. You will experience days when your inner voice, destructive as it may be, will be more persuasive then all the compassionate voices you hear from your support network.

I can relapse into old ways of thinking which tell me I can go it alone without help. If I hold onto old resentments and stop talking to others about these feelings, I can get myself in trouble. We receive some kind of payback from all our actions. Even resentments have a payback. Resentments keep people at bay, pushing away those we need in our lives. The voice of self-righteousness can come back to tell me that being right is all that matters, which further disconnects me from everyone else.

Taking the steps to heal our wounds by confronting the warden can be painful at times. This journey is paved with peaks and valleys. We will stumble at times. Stumbling and slips are tools for growth and learning; they are a part of the journey. The key is to stay on that path by putting one foot in front of the other.

Review the diagram of the old belief system below. Then, view the new belief system on the next page. It offers powerful freedom from childhood wounds.

Old and New Belief System Stages

The first stage of both the old and new beliefs starts with wounds and the messages that developed from these wounds at an early age. These messages create the inner voices that determine the fears in the second stage of both pyramids.

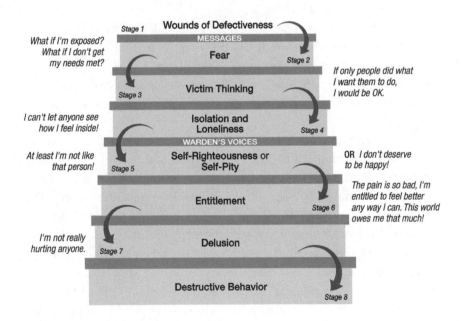

The Old Belief System

Guided by Wounds and Destructive Messages

What if I'm exposed? What if I don't get my needs met?

Stage 1 — **Wounds of Defectiveness**

MESSAGES

Fear — Stage 2

If only people did what I want them to do, I would be OK.

Stage 3 — **Victim Thinking**

I can't let anyone see how I feel inside!

Isolation and Loneliness — Stage 4

WARDEN'S VOICES

At least I'm not like that person! — Stage 5

Self-Righteousness or Self-Pity

OR *I don't deserve to be happy!*

Entitlement — Stage 6

The pain is so bad, I'm entitled to feel better any way I can. This world owes me that much!

I'm not really hurting anyone. — Stage 7

Delusion

Destructive Behavior — Stage 8

The key to freeing someone from the imprisonment of these wounds and messages begins in stages three and four in the New Belief System. This process starts by the person's willingness to stop the victim thinking in stage three of the Old Belief System.

With the aid of the warden's voice, victim thinking quickly gains momentum. It must quickly be replaced by healthy behavior, including reaching out to others and making a commitment to do written inventories on issues that create turmoil. If these actions are not taken, fears may build up to an overwhelming level and victim thinking will emerge. This may lead to a dangerous place called isolation. Written inventories bring us awareness of our responsibility. The connection we form with others allows our blind spots to be brought to the surface. Acceptance, forgiveness, and spirituality free us from the old recordings which kept us stuck in destructive thinking and behaviors. In time, the wounds in stage one slowly heal which creates less fear in the person. As the warden's voice becomes less frequent and more quiet we slowly free ourselves from the harmful roles we were set up to play.

The New Belief System
Guided by Healthy Information and Beliefs

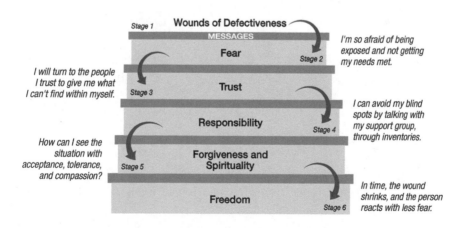

Chapter Ten:
The Most Precious Gift of All, Our Children

I cannot give my children what I don't have inside, just as my parents could not give me what they did not possess themselves.

ဆာ

Children need accountability and predictability from their caregivers in order to feel safe. Consistency in parenting enforces a child's self-esteem. Without consistent dependability the children feel anxious and uncomfortable, never knowing if their needs will be met. If children cannot count on this from their caregivers, they will become accustomed to chaos and create this chaos in their adult life.

The first time I went to a therapist, he asked me about my relationships. It wasn't until he inquired about my children that I became emotional. Thinking of my children reopened the wounds of my childhood.

Years later, I went to a workshop where I participated in a psychodrama. One therapist, using my infidelity to my wife as the subject and playing the role of my son, asked me why I was hurting him and his mother. He kept repeating, "Dad, how could you do this to me and Mommy?" Every time he said this, the pain cut deeper. My only thought was to hug and console this person, as if he really was my son. I was so taken in by the emotion that I approached him, and three other people were instructed to hold me back and let the role-play run its course. Nevertheless, I broke through their blockade, and I hugged the therapist, convinced he was my son, telling him everything would be OK. My only thought was to protect him and make him feel safe. I'll never forget this experience and the power it had over me. I'm sure this connected to the little boy in me who always wanted to be protected and loved by his father.

Children need caregivers who they can trust. It establishes

a foundation that allows the formation of a healthy belief system. This belief system permits the child to express his or her feelings without fear of losing the love of their caregivers. Love, they learn, is unconditional. If the child feels special, a sense of security will be established in his or her belief system. These caregivers do not necessarily have to be the parents. They can be grandparents, priests, rabbis, aunts, or uncles. Once they accept unconditional love, the children develop a sense of self-acceptance so that later, as an adult, they will have no need to wear a mask or medicate their feelings. Conversely, if love is conditional, children learn they are loved only when they are good. Unconditional acceptance is the key. Children whose needs are unmet don't usually act out until adolescence, at which time their handcuffs are loosened and their newfound freedom leads to destructive behaviors. Some of these behaviors are aimed at retaliating against their parents, although they may not be aware of it. These might include overspending, especially their parents' money, engaging in anti-social behavior, using drugs and alcohol, or doing the exact opposite of what their parents tell them to do. It is a subliminal way of torturing their parents.

As a parent, my new belief system was often at odds when it came to making important parental decisions. The most important action I could take for my children was to create a safe environment where they knew I would be there for them no matter what happened. I didn't want my children to experience the uncertainty and loneliness I felt as a child. A tool I use is to go back and think of the words I needed to hear from my parents when I was young. These words are not what I *wanted* to hear but what I *needed* to hear to feel safe and confident.

Today I make sure to share with my children all the things I wanted to hear from my parents. I tell them they are special and can confide in my wife and me without being judged. They don't have to be who I want them to be; they are free to determine their own destiny. Still, it isn't so much *what* I say as what I *do* that matters most. I can't expect them to ask for help unless I have the courage to seek help myself. I can't expect them to stand up for themselves if I'm failing to stand up for myself. The bottom line is this: *I cannot give my children what I don't have inside, just as my parents could not give me what they did not possess.* As a parent, I was no better or worse than my parents were; I could only draw from the information available in my belief system, just as my parents had done. Regardless of the love I have for my children, if my worldview is distorted, I cannot expect my children to view the world in a healthy way.

It is *healthy information* that must be passed on to our children. Four years after my father's death, my son had been chosen to play on an all-star little league team. My wife said, "Papa would have been so proud of you." His to-the-point reply was, "Papa was always proud of me." My son's remark showed that he felt accepted and loved unconditionally by my father.

My son's reality was much different than mine. My inner voice expressed a message conveyed long ago by my father, telling me that I wouldn't measure up unless I made lots of money. Similarly, messages from my mother told me that unless I made her happy, *first,* I wasn't good enough. These messages imprisoned me until I recognized how distorted my thinking was. As a result, I began to allow new, healthy information to replace the old. This new information originated from messages received from therapists, support groups, retreats, and many workshops. I learned it was OK to show anger in a healthy way. If I argued with people it did not mean I would lose their love. To disagree with someone was part of being human; it didn't mean the relationship was over. The new messages provided the building blocks for a more nurturing, self-accepting belief system. I soon recognized that the havoc of my former life was influenced by my old way of viewing the world. When I gave my children mixed signals it was because I was mixed up myself.

At one time, I didn't know how to express intimacy. Since intimacy meant pain as a child, I substituted destructive behaviors instead. As with my father, addictions came first, because they were linked to my survival. It was not because I was a bad father, but rather a discouraged father who needed help to get better. My problem was that I tried so hard to be different from my father that I went to the opposite extreme. I was unable to distinguish between acceptable discipline and parental abuse. Personal guilt prevented me from taking disciplinary action and establishing boundaries with my children.

Today I realize that avoiding conflict is just as harmful as creating conflict. There are times I will initiate conversations with my wife that are uncomfortable, yet doing so is healthy for our marriage. The one motivating thought that keeps me from avoiding this is the desire I have to stay away from going back to the person I used to be. Eventually my wife and I had to decide whether we each wanted to be married or not. If we decided to be in the marriage, this decision, like all other decisions in life, had to be followed by action. This meant getting outside help and doing what was necessary to heal our marriage.

I have stood clear of my old destructive behaviors and freed myself of the shame and self-hate I carried my whole life. In return, this has allowed me to see the damages caused by the warden's voice. While my inner voice is usually obvious, sometimes it is less detectable. I need people in my life to help me with that. I have this urge and need to control and protect my children from everyone and everything in the world. I don't want this message handed down to them, so that their fear of others paralyzes their lives.

I had an advantage that others didn't. This advantage stemmed from the realization that my childhood did not supply me with the tools I needed to be a healthy parent or husband. This awareness supplied me with the willingness to seek those that did have these skills. Eventually I gained insight and wisdom from other fathers. My identification with them brought unity and strength. We supplied each other with positive information that we didn't have in our childhood. The need to be liked by my children, combined with the guilt of my past, created situations in which saying no to them was excruciating. Simultaneously, I had to establish boundaries and talk to my support group when I felt like a cruel parent, especially when I needed to enforce consequences or properly enforce discipline. However, as was the case with my individual growth, the more I practiced awareness, action, and maintenance, the easier it was to say no to the voice inside my head. Willingness, open mindedness, courage, and desire to be the best parent possible got me through the tough times.

I remember the first time I told my father that I was going to get help for my compulsive gambling. He begged me to do something to cut the chain of insane behaviors that was passed down in our family from generation to generation. However, it was not only the behaviors that concerned me. It also was the character defects that were passed down. If I don't share my feelings in a healthy way, then my children won't. If I allow the warden to swing his bat at anyone who gets close to me, then my children will learn to do the same.

The Freedom to Cry in the Arms of One's Father

Several years ago we had to put our dog to sleep. Our oldest son was the same age as the dog, and he was very attached to her. As we returned from the veterinarian's office, I noticed our son was sad and withdrawn. I asked him if he was OK. He said, "I'm fine, Dad." I asked again, "Are you alright?" He replied, "I'll be alright." Instead of walking away, I hugged him. His tears started to flow as his grip on me tightened. At that moment, I knew I was providing my son a safe haven for him to cry. The message I relayed to him that day was it is acceptable to cry in the arms of his father. I never had a safe place to go as a child, but my son does.

Sometimes when I speak with my children, the feedback I receive makes me scratch my head. Accepting where my children are in their lives—instead of expecting them to share my views—can be difficult at times. As they get older, I realize that lectures only push them away. I try my best to keep identifying with my children instead of trying to get them to see things my way. They have their own path that will be paved with obstacles, and they will have the opportunity to learn from their mistakes. I can warn them not to put their hand in the flames, but I can't always keep them from doing it. Eventually, they will make a decision and learn to accept the consequences of their actions, their successes, and their mistakes. As a parent, one of the hardest actions to take at times is to take no action at all. If our relationship is healthy, they will return and share their failures and victories with us, without a warden's bat hanging over them.

Today, I teach my children to trust other people and ask for help when needed. It took me years to accept help, but if I pass this blessing to them at their young age, then I have given them a special gift. I do not always have to comply with my children's wishes, but I want them to know their opinions are heard. I do not want them to feel invisible. One of the ways my wife and I connect with our children is by taking one of them out to eat each week. Our intention is to have one-on-one conversation with each child, separate from the other children. They pick the place for dinner. When our children were younger they only wanted chicken nuggets. Now their tastes have become more expensive.

I share my weaknesses with them by explaining how perfectionism and controlling behavior hurt me. I tell my children about the value of mistakes, and how they can be used as a learning tool rather than a form of punishment. Today my children also see me pray. It is no longer something that causes me shame. Praying is not a sign of weakness; praying is a sign of strength because it takes courage to ask for help from a spiritual source.

As I allowed help into my life, it became easier to ignore the warden's commands. Today I have a chance to stop the victim thinking and voices of hopelessness that had been handed down from generation to generation. My children do not need to hear the warden's negative recordings that I grew up hearing. I am now free to love others and to be loved by my children and wife, the lights of my life.

Chapter Eleven: Forgiveness And Spirituality

The God of my youth was angry, resentful, and vindictive.
I often prayed, Please don't hurt my family for the actions I did.

ॐ‿ॐ

Everyone has his or her own beliefs and ideas about forgiveness and spirituality based on the way they were raised and their circumstances. The awareness of my wounds and the steps I took to heal became my path to recovery. The path is a lifelong journey. Along the way, I realized I would need to find a new solution when life did not go as planned. My deep wounds required a source more powerful than anyone, anything, or myself in order to heal. Spirituality, rather than addiction, would become my new solution when things got tough.
To find my spirituality, I had to better understand my Higher Power. My written inventories helped me identify the answers to these questions: What do I believe? Where did my beliefs come from? Why was I so afraid to depend on any authority figure, including sponsors, coaches, support groups, and even a Higher Power?

My inventories suggested the God of my youth was angry, resentful, vindictive, and not forgiving of my weaknesses. My childhood and adolescent perceptions were of a spiritual power who would never forgive me if I did not behave according to the standards taught at home and school. How could a Higher Power love someone like me with such flaws and imperfections?

My biggest misconception as a child was that I had to be a good boy to be accepted. That put me behind the eight ball. I was not good enough to be accepted. These beliefs continued from adolescence to my adulthood. My perception was that I would be punished for the bad things I did. My perception was that God would take it out on my children. When one of my children got sick, I thought God was punishing me through my children.

Praying until I Got It Right

My support group suggested that I face my demons head on. I asked members of my group how they renewed their trust in a Higher Power. One of the first suggestions was to get down on my knees and pray each morning. So, I prayed. It was difficult at first. It was not a priority. If I overslept, I did not pray. I prayed sometimes while driving to work, or after I arrived, and never on weekends. I figured God didn't work on the weekends anyway.

When I prayed, my mind wandered. But, I kept doing it even though I thought it was a waste of time. Several times I would be on my knees praying when my one of my kids would walk in. Embarrassed and ashamed, I would quickly stand up. I learned later through my inventories that, as a child, I thought asking for help and forgiveness was a sign of weakness. This false message was keeping me away from what I needed most to heal. I struggled to find my spiritual connection. Each time I got on my knees, I felt paralyzed with shame and fear.

I started praying by pleading for the willingness, strength, and desire to stay away from my addictions. Sobriety was the most important thing to achieve. It felt comfortable asking for that. If praying would help me stay away from my addictions it was more than worth it. I prayed to believe that God truly existed, which I sometimes doubted. I prayed to save my wife and children from my anger and to help me feel gratitude. I prayed for the confidence to believe that I deserved God's love. I wanted to believe this Higher Power would be there especially on the days I felt alone and disconnected. Some days it was hard to fathom that a Higher Power could care for someone who did what I did.

It took months before I felt comfortable praying. Slowly, some of my shame and self-hate began to dissipate. I started to develop a relationship with a Power greater than myself. Sometimes I could not wait to pray, as if I was a little kid waiting to talk with my father. I thanked Him for giving me the perseverance to keep going until I felt a connection inside. Then I asked Him to remove the negative voice that caused so much turmoil in my life. I did not ask for any material possessions. I asked for help to accept the world as he meant it to be.

I let this Power know about those who angered me or those who I feared. I also prayed when the warden was beating me down.

Spiritual Fuel

I needed spirituality, and began to find it when I prayed. This gave me a sense of connection. I kept a journal and wrote to my Higher Power, asking for guidance and strength. I kept returning to refuel my spirituality. The key was to keep the door open for spirituality to enter. Over time, praying became more comfortable and important to me. I even prayed on weekends. If I was behind schedule, I still prayed and went to work late. Praying became my priority, and God showed up as long as I continued to seek him.

Asking for Forgiveness

My spiritual growth had to include the reconciliation of broken relationships with others. First, I needed to forgive myself. Since forgiveness begins with healing, I began to recognize the pain I inflicted on others. I wanted to make things right with others. I could never know the full extent of the pain that my infidelity caused my wife. The best way I could show her my sincere regret was to be the best husband and father possible. I demonstrated to my wife that she and our family are my first priority. I stress this to the people I guide. We identify ways to show our spouses and loved ones that we are not the same self-centered people we used to be. We can help with house cleaning or taking our children to school. Calling our spouses during the day reminds them we care and that our thoughts are with them. The best example I can extend to my children happens by showing care and love to my wife. I make it a priority to take time during the week to sit down and discuss our feelings.

There are times when atoning and making amends are not welcomed and even rejected. That is when I surrender the outcome to God and make certain that I do not punish myself. The key is to learn from mistakes and not to repeat them.

Forgiveness

Why forgive others? In forgiving others, we free ourselves from the poison of resentment. The act of forgiving can be difficult because it touches the core of our being and childhood wounds. What benefit are we gaining by not forgiving? Does this give us permission to stay stuck in our old ways of thinking and feeling victimized by others?

The first step is to acknowledge the pain. We must admit that we are wounded. It is our responsibility to find peace by self-healing. Step Two is to understand why we are holding on to those resentments that hurt us. What old beliefs are creating this pain? Are we afraid of losing something, or do we expect too much from someone else? Is our victim thinking causing us to harbor old resentments? I must constantly remind myself that the people with whom I am angry owe me nothing. If I expect them to repay a debt they are not capable of, then I am setting myself up for predetermined resentment. Many of these questions are addressed when we do our written inventories on anger.

Once we can identify the source of our pain, we can share this information with our support group, rather than expecting the people who caused it to change. This is where the power of prayer will become evident. Failure to forgive permits our scars to fester and leaves us in a state of victimhood.

The better we feel about ourselves, the more we accept others. I now can recognize positive qualities in people, instead of shortcomings. This was once a foreign concept to me. In the past, I settled into the victim role. The role of victim allowed me to focus on what others were doing wrong, rather than putting the focus on improving myself. I felt comfortable focusing on their weaknesses, rather than their strengths.

Allowing compassion to enter my life became easier when I reminded myself that I once was an innocent child of God. While I made poor decisions, I am still worthy of forgiveness. This goes for the people who wronged me. I ask, "Can I relate to their fears and angers?" People who react in anger to others carry a lot of pain inside. I ask my Higher Power to help me see them in a spiritual way. My perception of people changed as I began to see people as individuals who were hurting, rather than people inflicting pain on me. I no longer carried the belief that their goal was to harm. Not everything in life is all about me.

Forgiveness can be nurtured by remembering that the people who harmed us were once innocent children of God. When I envision others as children, I have greater compassion, knowing they did their best with the belief system they inherited.

Forgiveness goes hand in hand with acceptance. I sincerely believe that acceptance is the key to problem solving. If we can accept people, instead of trying to control them, we will find greater peace inside. As we achieve self-compassion, we can be more empathic with others. But, if we are constantly at war with ourselves then we'll always be in conflict with others.

Forgiveness does not mean that we need to tolerate inappropriate or abusive behavior in others. Forgiveness frees us from the imprisonment of resentment, which poisons our entire being, disturbs our sleep, removes our joy, and injures our health. Resentment infiltrates all our relationships and can be passed down to our children and spouses. The power it has over our thinking cannot be ignored. Forgiveness is the only way to stop drinking the poison of resentment.

After I read my father's journaling in his cookbooks, I began to see him in a different light. As he wrote about his fears and the shame he carried his entire life, I saw him as a suffering, discouraged soul. He was not an indestructible, heartless person. He had to learn to trust others to help heal his pain, just as I did. If I could see him this way, then I could see others with similar compassion.

As I reflect on my past, I see how my perception has changed. In the process of healing, I had a choice. The choice was to change the world to fit my way of thinking, or to change myself. I chose the latter and discovered amazing results. No longer do I feel the world owes me something. I am grateful for the blessings that life has granted me. I do not allow others to dictate how I feel about myself.

There was a time when I hated to admit my weaknesses, but today I find comfort in this admission. I could not stop my compulsions on my own, and this defeat opened other doors of healing for me. The consequences of my actions ironically paved the path to intimacy, an emotion I never expected to experience. There was a time in my life when asking for help was an overwhelming task, but today I find it liberating. When I was finally open to receive help from others, it was like being given a beautiful gift. As the recipient of something precious, I felt it was my responsibility to share this blessing with others who struggle with their destructive behaviors and are not yet ready to trust others.

I had the opportunity to appreciate the true concept of forgiveness when a close member of my family had gambling problems. He was trying to stop his habit, and he needed employment. First, I sat down with my support group to discuss the matter of hiring him. I did not want to make a major decision without discussing it with them. All agreed that I would pay off his bills and deduct one-hundred dollars a week from his salary until he paid off his debts to me. He needed this lifeline immediately, because his electricity was shut off and he was about to be evicted. The arrangement with him started on the right foot; however, before the end of a year I sensed that he was in trouble again.

I knew something was wrong because he began to isolate himself. Then I discovered that he had taken my credit card and was using it. I fired him instantly. I yelled and screamed at him, and we came close to blows.

When I get this upset, I discuss it with my support group for advice. They agreed that I should have fired him, but they objected to my behavior. I thought that I was the victim and my anger and yelling at him was justified. But, his illness never entered into my mind. The group informed me that I owed him an apology for my rage. I didn't want to hear this but realized they were right. My ego was in the way. I had wanted him to apologize for his wrongs, but he was much too damaged inside to do this. I did apologize for my rage. At that moment, I felt great. I began to view this relative as a discouraged person who needed guidance, rather than someone who intentionally inflicted pain on me. What had been a horrible situation turned into to an opportunity to forgive. Forgiving him helped him to get back on track, which was only possible because I had left the door open to him with my apology. This lesson in forgiveness freed me from the prison of resentment.

My growth and improvement accelerated when I advanced from just believing in a Higher Power to fully depending on one. I now try to live in the moment by putting the pains of the past and the worries of the future into the hands of God. I seek guidance from God and from my support group. I am responsible to use the tools I learned to remove the anger and surrender to God. I now have a better understanding of what I can control and what I cannot.

Forgiveness is a spiritual process. To forgive others we must first forgive ourselves. It begins with self-acceptance and the belief that our Higher Power accepts our humanness, the good and the bad. As we forgive, we are forgiven. As we accept our shortcomings, we experience greater acceptance by others.

Three years after my father died I was shopping with my daughter who was looking for a Valentine's Day gift for her mom. As she searched for just the right gift, she spotted a pin with an angel. "That's it!" she said excitedly. When my wife opened the package, her eyes lit up. She asked if I had read the note that accompanied the pin. I said no, so she read it, causing my mouth to fall open with astonishment. The note said that this angel was born March 28, 1996, the date of my father's death. We stood there in stunned silence. That day I felt a spiritual presence that transcended my understanding.

My father had become a wonderful example of this spirituality. As I watched my father physically wither away due to his illness, his spirituality grew. He spoke of gratitude for the life he was given. My children always lovingly knew him as Papa.

Chapter Twelve: Parting Words

Falling off the path is part of the journey;
the key is to get back on the path if one stumbles.

ℰᴑℭℛ

As I found the willingness to work on my character defects I constantly asked my Higher Power, *Please protect me from me. Help me keep my feet where they should be, where my family would want them to be.* As I continue to grow in my recovery, my attitude on life changes. This doesn't mean that life becomes any easier, it just means I don't view life through the same distorted lenses I once did.

I always had a need to prove I was right no matter what the expense was and I still feel this way at times. When this occurs I lose my ability to listen, be empathetic, or have compassion for the way others feel. Today I ask myself, *Do I have to prove I am right, or is it better to choose closeness and listen more?* Also in the past I expected others to read my mind and anticipate what I was thinking. Today I work hard at expressing my feelings and allowing others to express their feelings.

My Wife

When my wife criticized me in the past, my initial response was anger. The warden told me she saw through my mask and knew what a pathetic person I really was. I felt defective as a husband, and when my wife triggered this belief I used anger to protect myself. The warden's voice, programmed by my victim thinking, blocked out any empathy I could have for her. As I healed and accepted my shortcomings, instead of letting the warden beat me up unmercifully, I found empathy and sadness for my wife's pain. As my attitude toward her slowly changed, she began to trust me enough to help her with her pain. My attention had to be centered on accepting her exactly where she was, not where I wanted her to be. She was healing from a wound

I helped create. As much as I wanted her to forgive my injustices immediately, I had to accept that her healing would not be on my time frame.

She had a right to be sad, and I was able to tell her that her pain also saddened me. I could support her feelings, even if they weren't the feelings I wanted her to have. The more I worked on my written inventories, the more I realized the distorted ways I processed the words I heard. This awareness increased my courage to ask my wife what I could do to help her with her pain. Many times I felt scared to approach her in this manner, because I was being vulnerable, an uncomfortable feeling for me. I had to keep showing her that I cared even if it meant leaving me open to hurtful remarks. I would get through these challenging moments by reaching out to my support group for help. They would be there to hold me up when things got tough. I could not control my wife's feelings about the past, and all I could do was stay connected to the right people and do the next right thing. In time, her feelings shifted from resentment toward forgiveness.

My Children

My children do not always do the things my wife and I wished they would. Like most children, they can be demanding at times. And when they express their anger at me I want to reflect that anger right back at them. At times in my childhood I felt invisible and would react with anger if I felt invisible as a father. The warden's bat swung away at anyone, including my children, for not allowing my voice to be heard. It brought to the surface what I was trying to hide the most: my feelings of inadequacy. At the same time, my false pride led me to believe I'm entitled to have obedient children because of all the things I did for them. All of these character defects are self-centered, because they make every situation a personal one. They all revolve around me. Also, my children's anger is not always my responsibility to change. Not every disturbance they have in their life is due to something I did as a parent.

My children needed boundaries and rules, not anger. These boundaries are a sign of love, not an act of abuse. They needed privileges revoked, not to be humiliated by their parents. If I didn't have the courage to say no to my kids, then I had to find this courage through the support of others. My children also needed healthy attention so they knew their feelings were valid. This did not mean that I had to do what they said. It meant I had to listen to their feelings, even if I disagreed with them. By doing this, it helped build their self-esteem, so that they never felt invisible as a child. Most importantly, I realized that my children did not grow up in the same insanity I grew up in as a child. I needed this awareness so that I didn't overcompensate as a parent, which at times could be as harmful as undercompensating.

My job is to create a safe place where my children feel free enough to tell me their feelings in a respectful way. The only way I could create an environment like this was to show them that I was sympathetic to their needs, instead of always providing a solution. By listening to them, instead of judging the situation, I was able to bring them closer to me instead of having a war over who's right or wrong. If I cannot let go of my anger, then it is my responsibility to pause and bring it to my support group. Before I said something that I would regret, I had to bring it to the people who know me best. I could process the negative feelings with them before angry words came out of my mouth. My goal is to be close to my children, help provide healthy solutions, and let them know I am there if they fall. By talking to other people in my support group, I used their experiences to bring healthy information into my family. As I proceeded to work on my written inventories, I started to focus on my defects and wounds, instead of trying to mold my children into the person I wanted them to be. As I accept myself with all of my defects, it made it easier to accept them for where they were in their lives.

My Mother

In the past, I was unable to say no to loved ones. There will always be people, especially family members, who create guilt and shame when I establish healthy boundaries. I need to learn that pain is part of growth, and sometimes the right thing to do can be painful. The key is what I do with this pain. Do I medicate the pain with destructive entitlements, or do I ask my support group to help me?

My new belief system taught me to look at the good in people. My mother is a terrific grandmother. She is sorry for many of the things that happened between us. She always loved her children but was living in a battlefield with my father. Without guidance, I would not know how to ask for forgiveness for her or myself. Even with the willingness to forgive, it can be a long journey requiring patience and paved with small victories. Forgiveness takes time, courage, and the guidance of others. I had to do the actions and trust the people who told me the feelings of forgiveness would come later. Eventually, I found gratitude for what my mother did give me. I found sadness, instead of anger, for what she couldn't give me. She was a person in pain; she was not personally trying to hurt me. If I wish leniency for my injustices, then it is only fair I find compassion for hers.

God

I used to get angry at God, as He allowed my father to die just when we were beginning to reconcile our differences. My victim thinking wants me to believe that God did this just to hurt me. I cannot play God. It is not my decision to choose when people should die. The feelings that I had when my father died were understandable; however, judging God, myself, or others triggers a sense of destructive entitlement within me, one of my enduring character defects. Instead of trying to figure out God's reasoning, I need to pray for acceptance of whatever his will is. Acceptance can be so difficult at times, but for someone like me resentment will only hurt those I love and myself. When I find myself fighting the things I cannot change, then I have to go to my support group and allow them to help me change the things I can. If I am trying to figure out why things happen the way they do, then I am putting myself in the position of God, a place I don't belong.

Me

Whenever I made a mistake, the warden made sure that all the shame of my past bubbled up, reminding me what a defective person I am. Whether it is work, my wife, my children, or anyone else, the guy with the bat on my shoulder was always ready to pound away. I always focused on the things I could have done better, never on my accomplishments. My business failures became my failures as a person. The belief that I failed as a child was so painful that I felt hopeless whenever I stumbled as an adult. My expectations of myself were so high that failure was inevitable. I was the one writing the script for myself and everyone else. If I couldn't control the future, then I couldn't trust that anything would turn out OK. If I did something wrong, the warden would immerse me in shame and inadequacy. Self-compassion and self-tolerance were hard to find when the warden was hitting me over the head with a bat.

After doing written inventories for years, I started to notice the ways my thinking was self-destructive. By becoming aware of these patterns, I was given the opportunity to see what I needed to change. Inventories revealed how I interacted with people; this helped me see that the problem was my thinking. As I continued to do my inventories, I realized that my childhood wounds distorted how I saw situations—and how I heard things. If I felt rejected, worthless, inferior, or disrespected in my relationships, it touched off a lot of fear inside of me. This fear protected the pain of feeling small inside. A wounded animal can become vicious when it is scared. I was emotionally wounded, and I can be vicious when I'm scared. By doing inventories I began to identify the wound and separate my wound from the actual incident which triggered it. This enabled me to see the ways I let these old wounds influence my reactions toward others and how I have often overreacted. This also gave me the opportunity to talk about the old feelings I kept locked inside for so many years. Talking about these wounds is a much healthier approach than feeling rejected and shutting down. Now, instead of denying or rejecting who I am, I accept the part of me that was broken. Through acceptance and a new belief in a power that I can depend upon, I began to heal. These wounds are deep and have been there for a long time. They will get triggered at times, and it is then that I must take the right actions. Exposing my weaknesses becomes easier as the need to protect myself decreases.

When I look back on the destruction I caused there will always be a part of me that wishes I could take back the betrayal to my wife and the time and money I took from my family. However, there is more to my story. The relationships I have with my wife, children, and friends today would not be possible if my destructive behaviors did not open up a door of opportunity for me. This door gave me the chance to view a part of myself that would have remained buried. I would sabotage intimacy or happiness whenever it came my way. Those destructive behaviors led me to a place of healing which is where I started to believe that I did deserve happiness and the love of others. I was chained to the warden's messages which constantly sabotaged my intimate relationships. The healthy messages I bring to my children today would not be what they are if I wasn't brought to my knees by my destructive actions.

Today, after twenty-seven years, I have gone back to school for a Master's degree in social work at Rutgers University. God indeed has a sense of humor. My warden and all of his voices were at it again, telling me I'll never get through this. As before, I put one foot in front of the other, while continuing to allow others and my Higher Power to hold me up on the days I felt inadequate. I do not have to walk alone anymore, unless I choose to.

In closing, I want to leave you with a loving message from my daughter. When she was eight-years-old, she asked my wife if she could speak with her grandfather, her "Papa," on the telephone. My wife dialed the phone and handed the receiver to my daughter. "Papa," she said, "I love you. I love you not because of the things you buy me or the places you take me, but because you make me feel good every time I'm with you." Never before had he felt such profound love. It is comforting to know that the message my father left my children was one of unconditional love, a message they can pass on to future generations.

Appendix A

ಐಲಡ

Readers may photocopy these inventory templates.

The Aggressor	The incident	My initial reaction, aided by the Warden's voice	Old fears and wounds re-opened by event	A more mature & compassionate reaction that addresses my role in the incident

Who were your caregivers?	Messages received from those caregivers	Our inner voice created from the messages	The behaviors our inner voice commands us to do	What we need from our support system

About the Author

Thomas Gagliano is a successful business owner and consultant who lives in North Brunswick, New Jersey, with his wife and family. For the past ten years, he has been a popular keynote speaker on recovery issues in the greater New York area. He has a Master's degree in social work from Rutgers University.

Gentle Path Books that May Interest You

A House Interrupted:
A Wife's Story of Recovering from
Her Husband's Sex Addiction

Maurita Corcoran

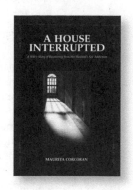

Maurita Corcoran's world collapsed when she
learned that her husband, a successful physician,
was a sex addict. She was suddenly submerged in a
world of painful choices about how to rebuild a life
for herself and her four children. This is an absorbing
memoir about forgiveness, resilience, and hope. With
the growing public awareness of how pervasive sex
addiction has become, this memoir answers the
questions that spouses must face in building lives of
self-respect.

280 pp
Trade Paper | $16.95
978-0-9826505-2-3 USC

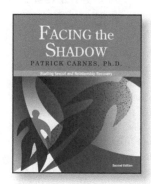

Facing the Shadow, Second Edition
Starting Sexual and Relationship Recovery

Patrick Carnes, Ph.D.

Dr. Patrick Carnes' ground-breaking book, *Out of
the Shadows*, introduced the world to his research on
sexual addition. *Facing the Shadow* is the innovative
workbook that helps readers understand how to begin
meaningful recovery from an often misunderstood
addiction. This book guides readers through the
first seven tasks in Dr. Carnes' researched-based
Thirty Task Model of treatment—the most respected
therapy model available for treating sex addicts.

325 pp
Trade Paper | $29.95
978-0-9826505-2-3

Mending a Shattered Heart
A Guide for Partners of Sex Addicts
Edited by Stefanie Carnes, Ph.D.

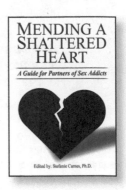

Hundreds of unsuspecting people wake up every day to discover their loved one, the one person who they are supposed to trust completely, has been living a life of lies and deceit because they suffer from a disease called sex addiction. Stefanie Carnes, Ph.D, brings together several authors to guide the reader through such difficult questions as "Should I stay or should I leave?" This comprehensive guide offers readers the best expertise available on how to begin the journey of personal recovery.

220 pp
Trade Paper | $19.95
978-0-9774400-6-1

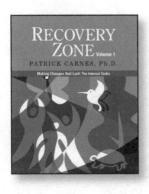

Recovery Zone, Volume 1
Making Changes that Last: The Internal Tasks
Patrick Carnes, Ph.D.

Recovery Zone, Volume One, picks up where *Facing the Shadow* leaves off, guiding readers through tasks eight through thirteen of Dr. Patrick Carnes' innovative Thirty Task Model. This book helps readers understand how to move beyond merely stopping addictive behavior. True recovery is achieved by learning to cope with difficult situations and emotions. Although there is no overnight solution for addictions, recovering people can learn how to achieve long-term sobriety by making decisions that suit their individual needs, devising a plan for living an optimal life, and becoming proactive leaders of their lives.

315 pp
Trade Paper | $29.95
978-0-9774400-1-6

Thirty Days to Hope and Freedom from Sexual Addiction

Milton Magness, D.Min.

Genuine healing is available to women and men who seek to restore their integrity and live in continuous sexual sobriety. Through a thirty-day approach, Milton Magness, D. Min., prepares readers for long-term recovery with essential advice on how to cope with isolation, dishonesty, secrecy, and what to expect from therapy.

290 pp
Trade Paper | $21.95
978-0-9826505-5-4

Surveying the Wreckage
A Guide to Step Four

John Leadem and Elaine Leadem

The course of addiction can cut a broad and deep swath through the lives of its victims. The Fourth Step, *We took a searching and fearless moral inventory our ourselves*, can be daunting, yet incredibly liberating. This guide helps the reader move through fear and doubt to successfully complete an inventory.

90 pp
Trade Paper | $14.95
978-0-9826505-3-0

Came to Believe
A Guide to the Second Step

Chet Meyers

In a world that seems increasingly violent, materialistic, and filled with problems, is it possible to believe in a Higher Power? Author Chet Meyers offers answers to this and other questions to help readers reframe their thinking on the nature of spirituality and faith. This is a thoughtful and nonjudgmental discussion of Step Two, *Came to believe that a Power greater than ourselves could restore us to sanity.*

90 pp
Trade Paper | $14.95
978-0-9774400-7-8

Connection and Healing
A 200-Day Journey into Recovery

Russ Pope, M.S., and Dan Green, Ph.D.

This guided journal provides two hundred days of inspirational writings on a variety of topics, including how to:

- reach out to family members and rebuild trust
- break habits of isolation and make the most of healthy connections
- experience the blessings of being truly known by others
- act in the true best interest of loved ones

430 pp
Trade Paper | $24.95
978-0-9826505-0-9

Hope and Freedom for Sexual Addicts and Their Partners

Milton S. Magness, D.Min.

Dr. Milton S. Magness offers sexual addicts and their partners step-by-step guidance on how to work through the phases of recovery. Readers learn about disclosure, celibacy contracts, relapse, and how to rebuild broken trust. This is a compassionate yet straightforward primer on how to end sexual addiction.

220 pp
Trade Paper | $19.95
978-0-9774400-5-4

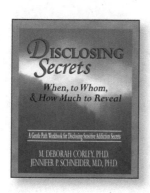

Disclosing Secrets
When, to Whom, and How Much to Reveal

M. Deborah Corley, Ph.D., Jennifer P. Schneider, M.D., Ph.D.

Nearly every book on addiction recovery discusses the need for "coming clean" with loved ones, but this is the only guide that exclusively addresses this essential step in revealing sensitive secrets. Readers will learn what, when, and how to disclose information related to sexual and other addictions, as well as who to involve and what (if anything) to tell children.

290 pp
Trade Paper | $23.00
978-1-929866-04-5

Open Hearts
Renewing Relationships with Recovery, Romance, and Reality
**Patrick Carnes, Ph.D.,
Debra Laaser, Mark Laaser, Ph.D.**

No relationship situation is hopeless. *In Open Hearts*, readers will learn how to overcome "coupleshame," fight fair, understand their family "epics," break free from the same old battles, form a spiritual bond, and renew their early passion. This book provides hopeful and helpful guidance on transforming one's most intimate bonds.

230 pp
Trade Paper | $19.95
978-1-929866-00-7

Ready to Heal
Women Facing Love, Sex, and Relationship Addiction
Kelly McDaniel

Author Kelly McDaniel offers women compassionate yet direct assistance on how to change painful relationships. Readers will learn how to address patterns of choosing partners who are addicted to sex and substances, how to stop being involved in serial relationships, and what to do about anger and other painful emotions associated with intimate relationships.

190 pp
Trade Paper | $18.95
978-0-9774400-3-0

Gentle Path Press

Gentle Path Press was founded in 1998 by Patrick Carnes, Ph.D., a pioneering researcher, clinician, and author in the field of sexual and multiple addictions. Dr. Carnes' goal was to publish innovative books and other resources for consumers and professionals on topics related to addiction, trauma, and brain chemistry. Gentle Path books provide readers with the best research-based materials to help repair the lives of individuals and families.

Dr. Carnes' cutting-edge research and writing became widely known in 1983 with the publication of his book, *Out of the Shadows: Understanding Sexual Addiction*. It was the first book designed to help addicts deal with their sexual compulsions, and to examine the tangled web of trauma, love, addictive sex, hate, and fear often found in family relationships. His research, work with patients, and writing have continued over the past three decades.

Experts and consumers alike have come to embrace Dr. Carnes' 2001 book, *Facing the Shadow: Starting Sexual and Relationship Recovery*, as his most compelling and important work to date. *Facing the Shadow* introduced readers to Dr. Carnes' revolutionary Thirty Task Model for beginning and sustaining long-term recovery.

More information on Gentle Path books can be found at www.gentlepath.com.

International Institute
for Trauma and
Addiction Professionals

Institute for Trauma
and Addiction Professionals

Dr. Carnes also founded the International Institute for Trauma and Addiction Professionals (IITAP), which promotes professional training and knowledge of sexual addiction and related disorders. Sex addiction affects the lives of millions of people worldwide, and practicing therapists are on the frontlines treating this epidemic. IITAP offers three distinguished certifications to addiction-treatment professionals: Certified Sex Addiction Therapist (CSAT), Certified Multiple Addiction Therapist (CMAT), and Associate Sex Addiction Therapist (ASAT).

More information can be found at www.iitap.com.

Excerpt from

Facing Addiction:
Starting Recovery from Alcohol and Drugs
by Patrick Carnes, Ph.D.,
Stefanie Carnes, Ph.D. and John Bailey, M.D.

Introduction

For all addicts, a moment comes when they realize they have a problem. In this moment of lucidity, it suddenly hits home how out of control life is. Then the old rationales and cravings rush back in to blur reality. Think of an addiction as being caught in a wild and dangerous white-water stream. Those flashes of understanding enable addicts to regain stability. If they act quickly, there is a chance of escaping danger before they are pulled back into the roiling and thrilling current. Others recognize their peril and know they must get out in order to survive, but the stream is too strong and those lucid moments too rare.

There are some who have reached a point where they refuse to be pushed around any longer. They seize the opportunity and with courage and work manage to find tranquil pools or beaches. They pull themselves out and discover they had forgotten, or maybe never knew, a calmer, more ordered world. With perspective they realize the last choice they would make would be to spend their lives in the raging river. If you are looking at this book, you may be wrestling with the problem of addiction to alcohol or drugs. If you are, this doesn't mean you are bad or hopeless. It means you may have a disease from which many have healed.

If you are a normal addict, you have probably made the following statements to yourself

- Nothing will help.
- I am overreacting to normal things.
- Others (my family, my boss, my neighbors) are overreacting to normal things.

- I am worthless and too damaged to change.
- The problems will blow over.
- I can stop if I just try harder (as opposed to trying therapy or recovery).
- I will be OK if I just drink or use less.
- I will be OK if I can be more clever about my use so I will not be caught.
- The reason I do this is because of (my spouse or parents or work or religion or culture) _____ (fill in the blank).
- My situation is different.
- No one will understand what I do (or did).

If any of those thoughts occur to you, you are exactly where you should be. This is what most addicts think when first beginning to confront their addiction. If you are starting to acknowledge your problem, this is significant progress. You may be open at last to the possibility that hope and healing can enter your life. If you have reached the moment where you know that your drinking or drug use is out of control, this book is for you.

Fortunately, there are now many books on addiction. However, this is the first book that takes techniques used with thousands of recovering addicts and uses these to teach you step by step how to break free from the raging current of addiction and make your life better. Decades of research and clinical experience have shown that breaking recovery into defined tasks makes it easier to leave the addictive life. As recovering people perform these tasks, they learn specific competencies with which to manage their problems. Taken together, these skills form a map for success. If they follow the map, they will reach the goal of recovery. If not, they will end up back in the whitewater.

This book is the tool many of us now in recovery wish we had when we started. It is intended to be used as part of therapy, either in an outpatient or inpatient treatment program. It is also designed to support a Twelve Step recovery program such as Alcoholics Anonymous (AA) or Narcotics Anonymous (NA). (Look for a listing of such support groups on page 256 of this book.) Please note, the content in this book is not intended to replace conference-approved materials that are published by AA or NA for use in Twelve Step meetings.

Both therapy and Twelve Step support are keys to success. Your internal addict voice will supply rationales for not doing therapy or Twelve Step work, such as

- Therapy does not work.
- Therapists are crazy or they would not be in the business.
- Twelve Step groups will not work for me.
- I can do this on my own.
- I do not like the therapist, the group, the program, the Twelve Steps, the people there, talking about myself, or _____(fill in the blank).
- My situation is different.
- No one will understand what I do (or did).

It is at this point that addicts must try to see what is really going on because they soon will be caught up in the rapids again. That is why our first chapter explores, "What is Real?"

We have personally known many people who have died because of their addiction, and we have heard the stories of countless others who have met the same fate. Delusion is the deadliest part of this illness. Those rushing rapids kill. If you are in a moment where you can see them, we invite you to come out of the river.